THE RESPONSIVE OFFICE

THE RESPONSIVE OFFICE

People and Change

Foreword by Dr Francis Duffy

Steelcase Strafor/Polymath Publishing

Published by Polymath Ltd, The Old School House, Streatley Hill,
Streatley-on-Thames, Berkshire RG8 9RD, England.
Telephone 0491–875032   Fax 0491–875035
on behalf of Steelcase Strafor, 56 rue Jean Giraudoux,
67035 Strasbourg Cedex, France
Telephone 010 33 88 28 90 13   Fax 010 33 88 28 31 78

First published in England 1990
Copyright © English Edition Steelcase Strafor 1990

First published in France 1989
Copyright © French Editions Nathan Communication 1989

Publisher and Managing Editor Charles Knevitt
Editors Fiona Gorman and Chris Bown, in collaboration with specialists from
Steelcase Strafor
Technical Editor Les Hutton
Designed by Chrissie Charlton & Company
Design Assistant Chrissy Levett
Diagrams by Chris Whear
Publishing Director John Taylor

British Library Cataloguing in Publication Data is available

ISBN 1 873224 00 1

Typeset in Linotype Joanna, Futura Medium and Futura Heavy
by Nene Phototypesetters Ltd, Northampton
Colour separations by AGP, Strasbourg, France
Printed by Grafedit, Bergamo, Italy

Front cover: photograph by Stuart Franklin/Magnum
Back cover: photograph by Brian Harris/Impact

Acknowledgements

The publishers would like to thank the following publications for research material reproduced in this
book: Facilities, a monthly journal published by Bulstrode Press, Porters North, 8 Crinan Street, London N1
9SQ (071–239 7786); Premises Audits, Bernard Williams, Bulstrode Press; Achieving Office Quality, a report of
international research on the nature of office quality and its relation to the processes of development,
design, procurement and management, edited by Peter Ellis, with contributions from Franklin Becker,
Francis Duffy, Peter Ellis, Barbara Ettinger-Brinckmann, Peter Jockusch, Andreas Kleinefenn and Sheena
Wilson, and available from Bulstrode Press; Orbit-2: Executive Overview, Gerald Davis, Franklin Becker, Francis
Duffy, William Sims (Harbinger Group Inc 1985), available from DEGW, Porters North, 8 Crinan Street,
London N1 9SQ (071–239 7777).

Thanks are also due to John Worthington of DEGW and to Robert Hodgkinson of the Department of
Surveying, Liverpool Polytechnic, for material that originally appeared in Facilities and to Healey & Baker,
Ernst & Young, and Adrian Finn for their contributions.

CONTENTS

FOREWORD

DR FRANCIS DUFFY

A WORLD OF OFFICES

Future historians had better hurry up. So far scholars have treated one of the most remarkable changes in 20th-century life with almost complete neglect. I refer, of course, to the rise in importance of the office – from being a trivial appendage to industry in 1900 to becoming the dominant economic and environmental experience of the vast majority of workers in the developed, and even in the developing, world today. The landscape of the late 20th century is the office.

You wouldn't guess this from the silence of the commentators. Nor would you learn from savants too bookbound to use their eyes that not only has the office grown vastly in importance but also that the office environment is increasingly subject to violent change in technology, in quality and in social significance. The evidence lies in front of us in the pages of this book.

THE CHANGING WORKPLACE

What are these changes? The first and easiest to grasp stems from technology; information technology is changing every aspect of office work, giving access to data and to powers of computation unimaginable a decade or two ago.

The second is more significant. Information technology has changed the social composition of the office, eroding the endless ranks of lowly clerical staff who used to inhabit loveless office sheds, replacing them with more highly paid, more demanding, more discriminating office workers who expect to enjoy choice at work.

Thirdly, these new office workers can use technology to grant themselves far greater freedom in the use of time and space; nine-to-five is as likely to become an anachronism as is dependence upon daily commuting, using 19th-century transportation to gain access to 21st-century technology. Office location is hardly a stable topic any more.

Fourthly, the changes are economic. Because change in the office is so constant, demanding and ubiquitous, far more money is now being spent on the relatively short life interiors of offices. It is in these interiors that restlessness is most easily accommodated. Conversely, the shell and the exterior of the office building are dwindling in both architectural and economic significance. Architecture, in this financial sense at least, is rapidly becoming a branch of interior design – the neutral shell within which the real dramas are played out.

THE OFFICE INSIDE OUT

What matters is the world within; the marvellous, dynamic, increasingly varied world of the office interior where so much that is significant now happens. Here is the stage for the boardroom struggles, the relentless financial calculations, the brilliant co-ordinative planning, the feats of intellectual and artistic creativity, the confrontations,

calculations and manipulations that are at the heart of modern life. The appearance and imagery of the office interior are more important than ever before. Given the new significance of these settings, it is becoming impossible not to design the office building from the inside out.

Added to this is the increasing diversity of office life and the unstoppable desire of those who consume, and sometimes suffer, the office environment, for more – more quality, more control, more freedom to change, more options, more technology, more privacy, more contrast. Such a need for individual solutions conflicts with any simplistic approach involving a global methodology, and instead requires individualistic interpretation.

CONSUMERISM IN THE OFFICE

Can individual consumer choice ever be provided satisfactorily? Until recently what has been sometimes called 'Fordism' (after Henry Ford) was the dominant economic mode in the West. Fordism depended upon mass production, mass marketing, and a mass audience, within highly planned, centralised and regulated Keynesian economies. Increasingly widely-diffused information technology, which is killing the old-fashioned clerical office factories, is equally putting paid to Fordism.

The new technology provides much greater potential for choice in both production and marketing and allows much more emphasis upon service and responsiveness to consumer needs. To fully exploit this, end users and facilities managers must be energetic and intelligent enough to realise that they can work with design companies to their own advantage. What is so encouraging about today is that office environment companies like Steelcase Strafor are not only willing to talk seriously with users but that components can be made, customised and redesigned as a result of their dialogue.

THE RESPONSIBLE WORKPLACE

Nothing valuable can be achieved without a combination of the resources of inventive and experienced office companies and the intelligence of demanding and calculating consumers. The design process must be explained and demystified – very much as is done in this book – and the consumer should provide feedback and direction, as some are already doing through routine post-occupancy evaluation of their projects.

Many great issues are emerging in Europe in the last decade of the 20th century:

● harmonisation of environmental and product standards

8

throughout the European Community;

- increasing awareness of what can be learned from the best international initiatives – North American, Japanese, Scandinavian, German;
- the increasing importance of 'green' issues in the workplace; avoiding deleterious products, conserving energy in component manufacturing and building use, sustainability in materials usage;
- rethinking the costs of commuter transportation, given the potential of information technology;
- the increasing power of better educated, more scientific facilities managers;
- the opening up of the design process to end users; and
- much more inventive use of the increasingly expensive resources of time and space.

These are the issues being addressed in a new multi-client study called *The Responsible Workplace* which follows in the tradition of the well-known Orbit studies (in the UK in 1982–3, and the United States in 1989). The objective of the new study is to work out what the office of the year 2000 should be like, given the critical social, economic and technological changes which are the context of this book.

Nothing can be taken for granted for very long in the world of work. A new kind of responsible workplace is certain to emerge as a direct consequence of addressing these vital issues – and perhaps even a new kind of responsible city.

This book, combining experience with consumerism, is intended to accelerate this process of learning, of continuous improvement.

9

Dr Francis Duffy is chairman of design consultancy DEGW, with offices in Glasgow, London, Madrid, Milan, Paris. He is author of the Orbit studies (1983 and 1985), *The Changing City* (1989) and *The Changing Workplace* (1990).

INTRODUCTION

Faced with worldwide markets, spectacular growth in the number of white-collar workers, and the Europe of 1992, the company of the future will need to be able to adapt to a series of both powerful and subtle changes in its business environment.

At the same time, industry's driving force moves ever further away from the concept of mass production, towards the idea of quality production – with an obligation on business to seek the pursuit of excellence. In addition, developments in information and communication technology, and organisational methods, will lead to radical changes in productivity patterns and even in job functions.

As a consequence, the individual's relationship with his work, his employer, and his peers, are all transformed. Whereas in the old office model the individual was traditionally ascribed a well-defined function within the division of labour, and was part of a permanent and stable relations network, the evidence shows that this situation no longer exists. All forms of business undergo more, and

more frequent, changes, soon prompting a complete reorganisation of internal structures. Job descriptions change, tasks are more diversified, responsibilities move around and are decentralised.

Such fluidity also challenges traditional hierarchies of authority, upsetting established chains of organisation. And information is required to circulate more and more quickly, leading to lateral decision-making in place of the vertical authority of old. With the breakdown of this established form of management comes a change in the relationships between individuals; staff can increasingly distinguish themselves by competence and flair, rather than by their rank and status. More and more, whole companies are perceived as single teams working towards the same goal, rather than as echelons of management dictating the work of employees.

Increasingly, the 'task force' concept is being used by business – smaller groups of employees are drawn together to work on specific projects. And more and more companies are moving away from employees performing discrete tasks as though they are just links in a production chain; now groups of people with complementary skills work together, pooling their expertise to achieve the same goals. Team members are able to ask for the information needed to complete the project from anyone in the company, no matter how senior; the emphasis is on the results of the exercise, rather than the means implemented to achieve them. Such an approach can solve difficult problems effectively, but it also has positive human consequences; task force members often form strong links that survive after the project is completed, and the set-up provides excellent teamwork training.

At the same time as this change in the working environment, individuals are increasingly reassessing their attitude to work. As people constantly strive for an improved quality of life, they also look for similar improvements in the quality of their work, and of their working environment. Technology helps to provide this, freeing man from routine tasks and giving him the opportunity for activities involving creation and decision-making.

So as the business ethos moves from quantitative to qualitative, individuals are reappraising their own values, seeking to achieve a better quality of life through a better quality of work.

To ensure that a company can meet these commercial and personal demands, it needs to analyse its expectations and goals, and those of its employees. Decisions need to be taken about the desired quality and quantity of production and the corporate image to be promoted, and steps must be taken to identify and satisfy the expectations of staff and others coming into contact with the organisation.

If a company is considering relocation, which is more appropriate: new-build or refurbishment, open-plan or cellular offices, task lighting or standardised fittings? How can the colour of the walls affect productivity and efficiency? In what way do pin-boards for cartoons and pictures increase an employee's sense of well-being at work? How important is a premises plan and what is the most effec-

13

tive way to draw one up? What is the role of the facilities manager and how can he help a company save money without sacrificing efficiency?

In order to assess these questions, however, and to determine the current and future needs of any company, it is important to look at the historical trends and innovations that have shaped modern requirements and dictated patterns of work. The move from the quill pen to the visual display unit has not happened overnight and the gradual changes along the way have all helped define the parameters of the modern office.

PART I

THE EVOLUTION OF THE OFFICE

From the stone porticoes of Whitehall to the glass and steel creations of architects Norman Foster and Richard Rogers, the office building has always formed the first impression of a company's image, as well as providing space in which business can be conducted. The structure and integration of a building within its surroundings help a business to satisfy its organisational, functional and cultural needs. And since the design of a building generally precedes and imposes constraints on the layout of work spaces, it is a fundamental element in the organisation of the working environment.

Although space management was for many years one of the most neglected areas of human endeavour, company managers now accept that an efficient, productivity-conscious business cannot compete without taking a serious interest in the working environment of its employees.

As every form of space planning and design says something about the company using it, office layout is increasingly being seen as a new way of projecting a corporate image – and it therefore demands a very high priority. With the pressures of a more rigorous economic environment, demographic changes that alter established social relationships, and new technology influencing patterns of work, companies are increasingly focusing on space planning.

Throughout its history, the organisation of the workspace has been based not just on considerations of efficiency and productivity, but on the desire to establish, and sometimes control, relationships between individuals. It is only natural, then, that the history of office buildings should closely follow the evolution of office work, reflecting the process of work and its social status. The history of work is closely linked with that of

Making a striking statement – Norman Foster's Hongkong & Shanghai Bank building

cities where it took root, concentrated and grew; buildings not only created premises for work to be carried out, they determined the social structure of the city at work.

The greatest change came with the Industrial Revolution, which was well under way by the 1840s. Britain led the world in industrialisation, and by this time less than a quarter of its population was dependent on agriculture. In the newly-industrialised society, the idea of office space was considered seriously, as the population gradually shifted to more urban pursuits and as industry grew in size and complexity. As markets opened up, and banking systems were developed, the organisation of work became more structured. The rationalisation of administrative activities in the new, larger companies, was accompanied by a formal, hierarchical system of organising offices which engendered the concept of the 'white-collar' worker. After first invading the home, or imitating its layout, office space subsequently developed according to the industrial model of production units: rationalisation, standardisation of operations, and task distribution.

THE SERVICE SECTOR

The Industrial Revolution also prompted, indirectly, the emergence of the service industry. Although the banking, legal and medical professions had existed for many years, they had not done so on a scale that demanded large, collective areas of office space: most professions conducted business in offices modelled on the domestic study. With industrialisation, however, the huge mill, factory and office block began to grow on the horizon and new services such as insurance were needed to protect mill and factory owners against the loss of their premises. Already, by the 1860s, the Sun Fire Insurance company ran a London office with 80 employees – housed in a building designed specifically for them.

Subsequently the service sector, which grew on the back of industrial growth, has become more important to the economies of the West, particularly in the 20th century as Third World countries have challenged the efficiency of industrial production processes. As a result, more and more people in the West are working in offices. The need for space which is not dictated, above all else, by the rigorous efficiency of manufacturing industry has also brought new challenges for designers, to meet the standards of comfort and the need for well-conceived office organisation and cable management that the proliferation of computers in the service sector demands.

Early offices followed factory thinking

In Paris, one of the first office developments was the Haussmann building, originally designed for habitation, with its vast representative areas, stuccoes and wainscotting, long corridors and rooms ranged in a line. These were later transformed into a long, monotonous series of uniform small offices. The building conveyed the image of high status, with clearly defined and protected space which was in keeping with the static and structured hierarchy of the people who worked there. Defined areas for staff doing specific tasks reflected their footing on the company career ladder. It was also, through its use of stone and symbolism, the embodiment of an inheritance linked with traditional values and the rigid urban scenography which the bourgeoisie had created to praise its own achievements.

LIGHTING NEEDS

The form of the office building grew directly from that of the factory. Initially, such buildings were conceived in a similar form to factory or mill buildings, with windows expressed as holes punched in heavy external walls. It soon became clear, however, that office workers required higher levels of natural light than those in a factory, so gradually the area of glass increased, creating ribbons of windows along building façades: in Britain, the abolition of the window tax in 1851 gave added impetus to the quest for more glass. Windows were not only large, they were set high up in the wall, and rooms had high ceilings to allow light as far as possible into the building. Office buildings remained narrow, to ensure no worker was more than 7m (24 ft) from a window. High ceilings

also helped to ventilate the workspace, along with opening sections in windows, but it was not until the 1940s that air-conditioning began to challenge natural ventilation.

Despite the size of the window, in many instances the bottom of the glass was positioned above eye level, as it was thought that views distracted employees from their work.

NEW TOOLS AND MATERIALS

Further development of administrative activities led to new work tools: the telegraph in 1844, the typewriter in 1866, and the telephone in 1876. The integration of these innovations into the working world gradually changed the nature of office work – and the physical organisation of the work space. As Le Corbusier, a leading designer of the modern movement, explained: 'The typewriter brought forward a standardisation of paper sheets used in offices, and as a consequence, of the size of all the files and of all pieces of furniture which contained them'. Typewriters also imposed a new work posture, which has challenged chair designers ever since.

17

Towards the end of the century, files and briefs, drawers and filing cabinets began to appear in business premises and real attempts at furniture design took place. Tambour door filing cabinets, for example, were designed to hide untidy documents – and have become familiar to generations of office clerks.

Wood (below) was challenged by the introduction of steel (above)

The strength of steel amply demonstrated

Wood was the most popular material for office furniture, as a German manufacturer's discoveries allowed it to be moulded for the first time, so that it could be used in the production of seats.

It was not until the beginning of this century that metal began to challenge wood's supremacy as the main substance for office furniture. However, its robustness and resistance, particularly to fire, soon gave it the edge.

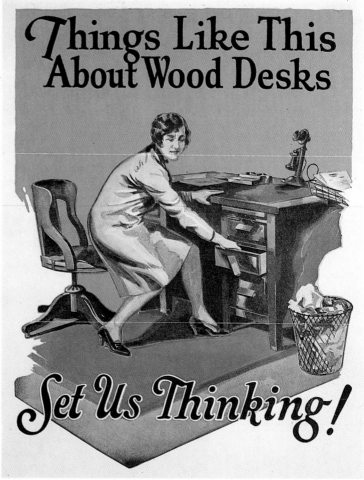

18

HIGH-RISE BUILDING

After the war, there was a huge increase in the development of synthetic materials. Nowadays, all these materials are to be seen side by side, with no one substance dominating. The office manager can choose according to function, ease of installation, cost and ergonomics, as well as looking at aesthetics and cultural values.

New materials have often imitated the ones they replace, in order to gain acceptance. At the beginning of the century, metal was painted to look like wood, and linoleum engraved to ape leather. Even today, sheet metal and plastic are finished in the image of granite, marble, cork and wood. In general, however, after a period of imitation, people begin to recognise the material for what it is worth and new production techniques harness the full potential of a material's technical, aesthetic and ergonomic characteristics.

It was in a completely different urban context from the early British forms of office working, however, that the strongest model of office architecture was to surface, towards the end of the 19th century. The development in the United States of new materials such as reinforced concrete and steel, the introduction of the elevator, the need for strong images to reflect corporate culture, and escalating land values all contrived to prompt the emergence of multi-storey office buildings. The high-rise block made its first appearance in New York, and then shortly afterwards in Chicago, after a great fire swept through the city's commercial district in 1871. From there, the development of the 'skyscraper' – a name which seems to be derived from the American colloquialism for a high-flying bird or a hit or tossed baseball – spread quickly throughout the world.

The multi-storey blocks marked the birth of the functional office structure, incorporating the early International style and turning their backs on historical forms of architecture. The first example was the Equitable Life Assurance Building which was completed in New York in 1870. At 39.6m (130ft) high, it was nearly double the height of its immediate neighbours and it also featured the first commercial use of a passenger lift. It was not, however, built around a steel frame. The first commercial building to use this construction method was the Home Insurance Building which was completed in Chicago in 1885 to a design by William le Baron Jenney.

The designs of these multi-storey buildings distanced themselves from the production process and created new work spaces – vast, colourless and highly mechanised areas – with each worker carrying out a specific task at a fixed position in fixed surroundings. These principles of work prompted the development of furniture better suited to the demands of function, rationalism and efficiency.

The high-rise block was to become a key focus for the modern movement, but its fascination was not achieved without causing some anxiety. Even Le Corbusier saw New York rising to the sky like some fierce, magical catastrophe. However,

19

for many years, precisely because of their qualities of excess, skyscrapers were to provide the industrial world and designers with their main vehicle for creation.

The development of highrise blocks has undoubtedly been one of the key vectors for change in building technology, bringing improvements in the resistance of materials and structure calculations, airconditioning, security and elevator systems. From the first passenger 'lift' – a miraculous contraption commissioned by King Louis XV at Versailles in 1743 for the private use of his mistress, Madame Chateauroux – to the first public lift at the London Coliseum in 1829, the elevator, itself only possible because of the development of electricity, made it practicable for business to be conducted on several levels of a building for the first time. As a result, a new image of work and hierarchy was created which dismissed the traditional, horizontal patterns of work. The centre became the top, imposing a more imperious stratification which organised the work process around the environmental space. The top and ground floors and the vertical circulation determined the company's new functional and symbolic relationships. These themes have been emphatically developed by high-rise projects to this day.

Sullivan's Wainwright Building

WAINWRIGHT AND LARKIN BUILDINGS

Architects Louis Sullivan and Frank Lloyd Wright set the pace in office design at the turn of the century. Sullivan's steel-frame Wainwright Building, completed in 1890 in St Louis, soared to 10 storeys. And a decisive point was reached when Wright's Larkin Building was completed in Buffalo in 1904. The architect's innovations were numerous: an integrated air-conditioning system, an atrium to increase natural lighting levels within the building, and the concept of all steel furniture. But most of all, Wright achieved a perfect match of interior and exterior, so that the envelope and inside fittings formed a harmonious whole.

Design developments continued in Europe, with the Dutch De Stijl movement in the 1920s and 1930s seeking simultaneously to come up with new furniture manufacturing processes and to improve working conditions. A series of vital questions which were to become a major preoccupation in the following years began to attract architects' and designers' attention. How do individuals work? How can we design offices that are able to meet their needs? Some large companies took an interest in these issues, with very significant results.

20

In Europe, the Thonet Company worked with architects Le Corbusier and Otto Wagner to improve the office environment, while, in the United States, designer Raymond Loewy teamed up with the Gestetner furniture company. Other notable contributions were made by Mies van der Rohe, the creator of steel tube furniture, which was used increasingly in offices both in Europe and the United States, and by the Bauhaus, the veritable design laboratory of the 1930s, whose innovations in office design became particularly apparent after the war. It was then that some of the most prominent members, including Walter Gropius and Marcel Breuer, moved to Britain and then on to the United States and founded the New Bauhaus.

Chaise longue by Marcel Breuer

After World War II new trends emerged as the perceived value of office work changed. Offices were increasingly organised on the principles of openness and communication, in contrast to the dull, oppressive rigidity of the office pool. The work of architects Sullivan, Wright and van der Rohe continued to move architectural development of the office forward.

EUROPEAN OFFICES

As a model, the high-rise office building was in symbiosis with American space patterns. Its transposition to Europe, however, had to face a strongly sedimentary urban fabric. How can one construct the city and work places if one cannot build on its existing foundations – on that segment of history which has become obsolete, unable to adapt to people's needs and to the forms which best express those needs and new aspirations?

Nowadays, we know only too well the kind of answer that was given to this question during the 1960s, a time of euphoric reconstruction and marked economic growth. Huge renovating operations took place, in many cases without much discernment and in an erratic and systematic way, so that the city one was supposed to be rebuilding was destroyed. Business centres thrived away from saturated city centres, and high-rise buildings of common-place architectural quality, with equally undistinguished plazas, rose up. These were the results of briefs which were concerned almost exclusively with maximising office space and economic productivity, so that the finished product was often a tall block with thick, external walls and little natural light, imposing an impersonal and introverted working environment.

However, while architects were often producing unremarkable buildings, a new awareness of people's needs was beginning to emerge inside the offices. During the 1950s and 1960s, with the worldwide proliferation of office development, proper working areas were created in which the concept of interior decoration began to gain credence and increasingly chairs and arm-chairs were mass-produced. The ergonomical approach developed to try to adapt work spaces, as well as equipment and furniture, to users' needs. The science of space management was coming up with innovative solutions to suit customers' needs, and office space consultants thrived. They identified the important operations and dynamics in the office, as well as the various solutions available for furniture and equipment in terms of function and aesthetics. The concept of the workstation evolved, with its progressive use of systems and modules, reinforcing the already predominant emphasis on flexibility.

Mies van der Rohe set the pace with steel furniture

21

An early American landscape office

22

In 1960, for example, the 'landscape office' emerged, brainchild of the Quickborner team which was founded by the Schnelle brothers in West Germany. Space was organised around the movement of paper and data and the greater spatial freedom and need for flexibility that the changing economic and human environment demanded. While the landscape concept was in its time an innovative and audacious progression, it became used as an excuse for densely-populated offices, and later showed other weaknesses. Staff in landscape offices could often become anxious as their need for privacy and a defined personal territory was sometimes not met. The landscape office seemed unable to satisfy the human ingredient of the office; but it is this ingredient, man himself, that subsequent systems have focused on.

The fact that high-rise offices came to represent dehumanised work made them widely resented. It was not until technological innovations and tools dictated new forms of work organisation that a real office architecture was developed which could meet people's needs and help the company blend with its environment. As a result, and as the work of Foster, Rogers and Italian architect Renzo Piano bears witness, the multi-storey block has a place in the urban landscape, and work can rediscover its human content.

THE ROLE OF WOMEN

Another major influence on the design of office space came with the emergence of working women. While in the Industrial Revolution both women and children were exploited by factory owners keen on new sources of cheap labour, the image of the woman at home still persisted. In Britain, the suffragette movement helped to establish the radical idea that a women should be treated as equal to a man, and the absence of men during both world wars inevitably meant that women

had to take on work in male-dominated industries. From that time, for many women, the chance of further education and a natural progression to a working life became an opportunity that their mothers had been unable to experience.

Further changes in attitude have helped to dispel the view that a woman's place is in the home, with the result that, in many sectors, women make up about half of the workforce. The service sector has proved itself particularly attractive to women employees, not least because service companies have traditionally required large armies of clerical staff. While employers can be criticised for regarding such jobs as offering little career progression, such employment has suited many women who combine office work with motherhood. The wide availability of clerical work means that a woman taking a break from the office can easily return to a similar position when her children are older.

From their first appearance at work as an alternative to men during the wars, women are increasingly being seen as the main source of the British workforce. This attitude will prevail well into the 21st century as demographic changes have reduced the number of young people in search of work and made it vital for employers to tempt women back to work after they have had children. This, too, is bringing its own demands for flexible working, job-share schemes and the provision of creche or nursery facilities in many companies. Not only do employers increasingly have to consider the health, wealth and happiness of their staff, they must now also consider their children if they are to win and retain employees.

23

Semi-enclosed space provided by system furniture

POPULATION by sex, age and marital status, 1986
England & Wales

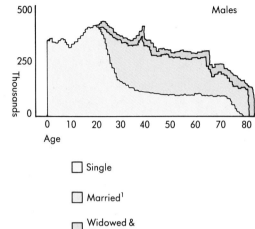

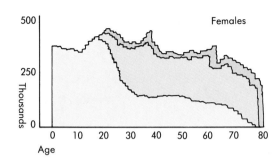

☐ Single

☐ Married¹

☐ Widowed & divorced

¹ includes separated people.   Source: 'Office of Population Censuses and Surveys'

24

The reliance on women workers has also undoubtedly influenced the development of comfortable office environments, as employees bring with them the experience of creating such environments at home and the expectation of maintaining such comfort at work.

NEW TECHNOLOGY

Computers, too, have had a dramatic influence on the office. Initially bulky, complex and expensive, they demanded their own specialised department in an office – and were often put on display by companies keen to show off their technological prowess. Such machines had a central drive unit, with users throughout the building connected to it, demanding not only the installation of a new régime of wiring, but also the need to find desk space for a video terminal and keyboard.

Individuals have a high expectation of comfort at work

Computer terminals have a dramatic impact on office planning

Improvements in the technology have reduced the size, complexity and cost of such machines, to the point where many companies have now dispensed with the central control unit and the 'computer department' altogether. Instead, individuals have stand-alone units on desks, which may be linked into a small network with colleagues in a particular working group. The need to adapt wiring has therefore changed, and individuals have closer control over their own work tools.

A recent survey by commercial agents Healey & Baker reveals that there is now an average of almost one visual display unit for every two office employees in the United Kingdom. Raised floors and suspended ceilings have become the most popular solutions for dealing with the huge lengths of cabling this hardware has produced. Not only has the rise of the computer altered individual work practices, the enhanced and extended line of communication it provides has also meant that, in some cases, employers have been able to be less demanding about their choice of location.

In an attempt to meet the challenges and overcome the constraints of the historic, urban context, several programmes have been tried outside the city. Designers have attempted to recreate in abstract the conditions of a real urban framework; and the new balance between verticality and more generous hori-

Wright's Johnson Wax building –
harmony at work

zontal plans has brought with it a long-forgotten vocabulary of streets, squares, gardens and green spaces. Companies can now replace the concept of a building with that of a town, where empty spaces generate new shapes and architectural flows, and the emphasis is more on communication than on function.

Healey & Baker found that the most outstanding change in the office sector between '1986 and 1990 was the emergence of a new generation of buildings away from the city centre. Congestion in cities, rising levels of car ownership and relaxed planning laws have all contributed to a thriving market away from central business districts.

Such buildings tend to be lower and narrower so that users can enjoy better contacts with the outdoor environment. After the fascination of high-rise offices, and the more or less successful attempts at relating them to the urban framework, a new concept emerged which saw the office as a tool, able to unite internal organisation and external activities with the company's economic and social environment.

JOHNSON WAX BUILDING

When, in the mid-1930s, the chairman of the Johnson Wax Company asked Wright to design the company's new administrative head office in Racine, Wisconsin – both the building envelope and the internal fittings – he was asked to design no less than a modern cathedral. Wright had previously undertaken the Larkin Building in Buffalo, where he designed metal office furniture as well as the building itself.

The completed work was strongly allied to its religious metaphor, with a large nave-shaped hall containing gigantic columns which fanned out into a corolla. Wright's concern for

26

brightness within the building led to top lighting, with Pyrex tubing forming a series of strips and translucent beams. The architect then collaborated with the Steelcase Company, a manufacturer which was already well-known for using modern materials such as metal tubing, to produce furniture and fittings which were in harmony with their surroundings. Metal tubing, which was only developed in 1920, was still considered an avant-garde choice for furniture.

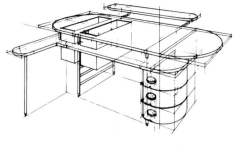

A range of desks complemented the building

28

Nevertheless, Wright's designs for Johnson Wax became among the most famous office furniture in the world, both for their revolutionary design and because they bore the stamp of their creator.

Innovation came with Wright's choice of colour for the furniture and with the alliance of shapes: cherokee red was chosen to match the brickwork, steel tubes echoed the Pyrex tubing of the lighting elements, and the curves of the seating evoked comparison with the pillars and corollas.

First and foremost, however, Wright's design was a system. He designed not just a desk, but a series of nine versions, each corresponding to a specific function and work situation. Although ergonomics was not yet a recognised discipline, its spirit was present. Each unit integrated the work tool – in particular typewriters and filing trolleys – and facilitated handling operations.

The way in which the components were distributed in the building was arranged on the same principles, seeking to create a working environment which unquestionably combined aesthetic and operational qualities to everyone's satisfaction.

PART II

CHALLENGES OF THE MODERN OFFICE

For a company to thrive in the increasingly competitive and growing international marketplace, it needs to consider three key areas which determine the decisions to be taken about a new or refurbished corporate headquarters or office.

The building must help rather than hinder the organisation in performing its business functions. The company must be able to tackle these tasks within the economic constraints of a business plan. The building must satisfy the needs and expectations of the people working within the organisation and those coming into contact with it, as well as satisfying the organisation's requirements of those people. In addition, the company's investment in an individual's workspace must match that employee's contribution: equipping low-grade clerical staff with complex computer equipment may well be a waste of resources.

1 ASSISTING THE COMPANY TO DO BUSINESS

The location and internal organisation of a building are vital factors determining the success of a company. If you locate your financial services firm in west London when your main potential clientèle operate in the City, the decision may hinder rather than help your business. Equally, if you place staff in introverted, closed office layouts when their work demands group decision-making or creativity, the decision could stunt productivity.

With the coming of increased international opportunities with the single European market, it is particularly important for companies to identify their position, metaphorically, in the marketplace, and reflect it, physically, in their choice of building. Offices can, and should, mirror an organisation's corporate culture, both in terms of the signal they give to the public – affluence and efficiency, for example, are often

suggested by impressive reception areas – and also in the message they give about the structure of the group. Does the layout of the building suggest a traditional, hierarchical philosophy or is it hinting at a more horizontal, equal style of management in which staff are encouraged to participate in decisions? These considerations demand a response from a company considering its location, and the penalties of failure can be absolute.

31

It is also no longer adequate for a company to regard its building merely as a container for its activities; the bricks and mortar, or concrete, steel and glass, make a key statement about an organisation's image and status. A first impression can only be made once, so it must be the right one. A company's building should be seen as an asset rather than an overhead. The message is not, however, just for the public, but also for employees. To attract and retain trained staff, one of the fundamental resources of any organisation, it is essential to ensure that they are happy with their working environment – and nowadays staff have higher expectations about levels of comfort and personal control than ever before.

CHOOSING THE MESSAGE

Business has found, in the modern office block, an ideal opportunity to express its corporate culture to the outside world. The establishment of a clear identity is an essential task in a growing and competitive market-place, and one which can improve communications with customers through logos, slogans and a strong corporate image, and with staff via magazines and internal meetings.

Everyone agrees on the importance of this concept and its economic impact, but talking about 'company culture' means defining the particular characteristics of a company through its organisation, values and symbols, and pinpointing the image it has of itself and the signal it wishes to give to others.

The organisation of space plays a symbolic and prominent role in defining a corporate character; as an emblem, it helps create a good or bad corporate image. And the building, through its siting, architecture and landscaping, must reflect the company's image; offices, through space distribution, de-

coration and furnishing, reinforce the cultural message. They are, in a way, the company's business card.

Cultural signals are there for the employees too. The signs, logos and symbols within an office are tools which are shared by members of a team, helping to create a link between individuals. It is therefore important that those who help create this culture on a daily basis recognise its values and coherence, and approve its modes of expression. Space, as one of the languages of this culture, becomes a tool by which the company can sell its own image to its employees. If a good brand image is conveyed to staff and customers, then it should also motivate the best recruits on the employment market. Furthermore, a message of intimacy and comfort conveyed through the organisation of an office can help individuals to feel part of a community when their specific task may seem more abstract because of its repetitive or isolated nature. The introduction of new technology, in particular, might reduce direct human contact and demands renewed effort to make employees feel part of a team.

Never before have firms needed to be so watchful of their image and values, and of the approval of those who, for a time, take part in shaping their destiny.

Clear messages for visitors and staff

33

CONVEYING THE MESSAGE

Architecture and interior design can give out several and sometimes ambiguous corporate messages. On occasions the message received can be quite different from that intended by designers and decision-makers, and the company should be careful to avoid any possible misinterpretation. One company, for instance, attempted to design its office buildings to express the organisation's search for quality, its wish to enhance the environment, and its responsible attitude to the community. However, its attempt to blend in, using architectural elements such as brick and pitched roofs, was ridiculed by locals who compared it with a fast food outlet or furniture store – a misinterpretation which transmitted an entirely negative message. Ideas must also show a desire for truthfulness and balance, expressing the culture without shyness or exaggeration. Too much luxury or, conversely, inadequately equipped and decorated offices, counter such ideas of openness and could jeopardise the confidence of employees and customers. Banks, for instance, have to strike a balance between assuring the customer that they are a

Generous use of space gives a relaxed feel

secure financial institution – by having premises with an air of permanence – and avoiding any suggestion that customers' money is being wasted on providing their own employees with lavish working conditions.

Adopting modern principles does not, however, mean espousing uniformity. While most companies will adopt a sober approach, others will find their culture best expressed in a more audacious and innovative manner. Classicism may seem appropriate for an insurance company, while a broadcasting firm may feel originality promotes its culture better. It is important to bear in mind that no two companies, however alike, will have the same culture or communications strategy. Where one firm expresses a desire for centralisation and authoritarianism, another may wish to decentralise, promoting individual responsibility and conviviality.

Any first step must involve agreement on the message, as spaces, like architectural forms, are not interchangeable, and structures adapted for one set of requirements may not suit another. The message, imparted by a well-conceived space strategy, should promote corporate identity and demonstrate its originality.

34

Architecture and image are inseparable

CHOOSING A BUILDING

Most businesses start space planning with an open, rectilinear view of the floorspace at their disposal. The evolution of speculative office development has ensured that such floors – occasionally punctuated by supporting columns – are available for sale or lease in a variety of sizes and locations. Offices of this kind however, bring with them standardised finishes, selected by the developer as appealing to a wide range of potential tenants. With an increasing number of tenants expressing dissatisfaction with this approach, some offices are now offered on a 'shell and core' basis – the structure is complete and services such as electricity, lifts and air-conditioning are installed, but nothing more.

Following on from this is the concept of the 'intelligent' building. This promises to help maintain, by automated controls, a satisfactory working environment, and to provide the flexibility to cope with changing requirements for office machinery. To date, while concepts such as raised floors have been adopted – allowing office floors to be rewired easily – the true intelligent building remains a concept rather than reality.

Something is being done, however. In 1982 – Information Technology Year – a group of British architects and office systems experts realised that the stresses information technology

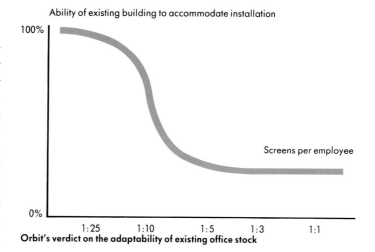

Ability of existing building to accommodate installation

100%

0%

Screens per employee

1:25 1:10 1:5 1:3 1:1

Orbit's verdict on the adaptability of existing office stock

was imposing on office buildings were of a type previously confined to high-technology industry and highly specialised information-based companies. They undertook a project that broke new ground in linking specific building characteristics – for example, a building's depth, floor to ceiling heights, location of cable trunking – with the ability of the building to accommodate the new information technologies. Their conclusions

were published in 1983 as the Orbit report (Organisations, Buildings and Information Technology).

A follow-up to this report, Orbit–2, was published in the United States, with a different goal: to develop a systematic, comprehensive building appraisal methodology which would allow buildings to be rated and matched to specific organisations.

35

First impressions are vital

Orbit suggested that existing buildings could not cope with new technology. It concluded that even installing one screen between three people is possible in only 30 per cent of existing buildings. For the necessary hardware to be installed, buildings need vertical cableways, which should be wide, simple and straight, and floorspace for additional power and connection blocks, which may amount to 2 per cent of available space. Computers also need protection from excessive voltage, power cuts, and parasitic frequencies.

The amount of equipment needed in an office is also growing, with the introduction of modems, printers, disk drives, etc. Although the thermal properties of much of the equipment have been reduced, any office will still need efficient and decentralised air-conditioning and ventilation systems. A microcomputer throws out as much heat as two people and, when linked to a telephone or modem, it can bring with it a mass of cables which must be channelled, while still allowing mobility and accessibility.

The installation of a computer network must also leave scope for the equipment to evolve. One can expect a proliferation of electronic data processing hardware in the next few years, but it is hard to anticipate the features that may need to be incorporated, so offices must be designed to be as adapatable as possible, without sacrificing efficiency on a day-to-day basis. Although new technologies are likely to become less demanding, there will still be a mass of cables and access to the various wire networks will still present a major technical problem.

For many companies, however, although many of these questions will have to be considered, financial considerations may dictate a slightly less ambitious approach. Refurbishment of existing premises may provide the solution. Nevertheless, while this may seem a better commercial response when compared with the cost of finding a new building, choosing lighting and flooring and other fitting-out decisions, the cost of disruption of business activities may be more damaging. Settling for refurbishment, which is increasingly popular in today's rigorous economic climate, may mean tackling only the more superficial areas of reorganisation, as the cost and disruption caused by redesigning the air-conditioning, for example, may be prohibitive.

The need to realise the potential of built assets often leads companies to convert premises not originally intended for office use, in order to meet their needs for administrative space.

Such a move can work very well, but it may involve alteration and restoration to adapt the building for its new use. In creating the office space, it is usually worthwhile minimising the amount of construction work and instead using careful fitting-out to achieve the required office layout; not only does this approach save on construction costs, but it means the building is more adaptable should future change be necessary.

The Lohr company, a haulage company in eastern France, used refurbishment to provide an overflow space for its head office premises. The company's existing office was housed in a listed building which planners would not permit to be extended or redeveloped, so instead the additional space needed was created in a barn at the rear of the site. The structure, which had stood unused for 40 years, was completely renovated and fitted out to provide workspace for administrative staff. As a result, the company avoided a disruptive relocation, and was able to keep all its head office staff on one site.

Lohr's successful refurbishment, interior (left) and exterior (right)

TRADITIONAL FEATURES AND NEW PARAMETERS

Although data processing technology is changing constantly, many features of the traditional office are still in evidence. Paper may be used less now to prove the existence and enable the exchange of information (one can read information in other forms), but it is still the prevailing medium for data from photocopiers and computers. A recent survey pointed out that computer printers in the United States use enough paper each day to encircle the Earth 14 times. The evidence seems to suggest that paper consumption will continue to rise until the end of the century, when it will start to level out. Since the market for electronic printers has never been so strong, paper is likely to remain a feature of offices for some time, so space must be found for it.

Working practices are changing too, as office equipment advances, as is the way in which individuals communicate with one another, both within the same office and between individuals in different offices of the same organisation.

Allied to changes in office hardware is a change in the way staff perceive their work. Increasingly they are motivated by factors other than money, such as shares, health insurance and a comfortable working environment.

INFORMATION AS RAW MATERIAL

Of course, paper is not the only medium; the various requirements of information exchange have prompted the use of chemical, magnetic and optical media: microfilms, tapes, diskettes, etc. Whether data is presented vocally (by telephone or radio), numerically or pictorially, it can now be picked up, processed

and distributed through independent centres far from the source. Electronic networks can dispatch information and services to companies and even to individual workstations and such shared services give access to a wide variety of databases.

Since information is a raw material which is a major source of wealth, increasingly sophisticated tools and methods are being used to process it. The exchange of information has become a very important element of office life and since an employee's level of access will depend on his job status and responsibility, the design of his workstation must reflect its place within the information network.

Paper – a persistent problem

THE INVASION OF NEW TECHNOLOGIES

As data processing has been transformed by office automation, so the office workstation has had to change. Information technology was comparatively expensive until about 1970, because of the cost of equipment and the need for specialists to install it. Most companies formed computer departments

and computer knowledge was confined to these staff. However, this elitist, centralised policy was gradually reversed over the next decade, because of the emergence of mini- and microcomputers. This equipment, which can be installed at most workstations, allowed the fusion of information and telecommunication techniques. At the same time, the cost of hard and software dropped, making it a reasonable outlay for more people.

The emergence of this new technological environment has meant the simultaneous growth of microcomputer and mainframe information; the creation of a large number of more user-friendly programs; the opportunity to connect various types of office equipment; and the installation of communication channels between various pieces of equipment and sites. As a result, companies can rely on better service and performance to pick up and process information more quickly.

As has already been mentioned, it is going to be some time before paper disappears from offices completely. Classifying, storing and filing operations will still have to be performed, so the office must be planned to cater for them. So, although one can expect computers to improve company efficiency, the hardware creates its own constraints affecting office space. The survey carried out by agents Healey & Baker in 1989 suggests that 46sq m (150sq ft) needs to be allowed as usable space for each member of staff. This is much higher than previously allocated and is largely due to the increased space requirements of electronic machinery. People need more room for their workstations than was estimated a few years ago and for the piles of documents which still exist in the computerised office.

Computers allow a company to survive, thrive and expand. Early on, the introduction of computers into the office was limited to carrying out low-skill work that was boring for humans. Now, however, it has become clear that the computer can carry out some work better than people, for instance in fields such as invoicing where a chain of events has to be carried through rigorously. At the same time, the savings in both time and cost that computers create can make a company more competitive. Nowadays the computer increasingly belongs to the whole communications system, and is completely integrated in the manufacturing and administrative functions of any company. For staff, the computer has become a tool, giving them options that were previously not available; computer-aided design, for instance, allows its user to view prototype products in a way that was previously impossible.

The size of computers has diminished as their capabilities have increased

NEW ORGANISATIONAL PATTERNS

The structure of employment is undergoing a fundamental change. The growth of direct communications between computers, and continuing improvements in the quality of optic and speech reader equipment mean fewer people will spend less time finding and relaying information.

The increasing use of part-time contracts, subcontracting and working at home, are also affecting office organisation. This change in the nature of jobs, especially low-qualification jobs,

COMPUTER USE

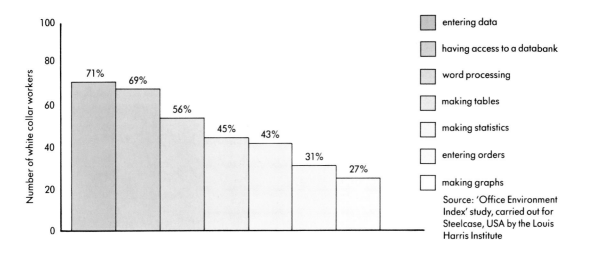

- entering data
- having access to a databank
- word processing
- making tables
- making statistics
- entering orders
- making graphs

Source: 'Office Environment Index' study, carried out for Steelcase, USA by the Louis Harris Institute

is gradually leading to an increase in the number of highly qualified specialists and executives. As a result, group mobility, development of project work and the flexibility of functions are all accompanied by a diversification of tasks and decentralisation of responsibilities. In some companies, workspaces are organised according to the tasks carried out rather than the user's status and, as a result, certain workstations can be shared. This approach has been adopted for sales personnel at IBM in Japan, with one group using the workstations in the morning while their colleagues are out with customers and the other group returning to the screens in the afternoon. However, although the changes in technology have allowed some activities to become more 'delocalised', this advantage may have limited appeal, as employees tend to like the camaraderie and social interplay of office life. Improved office automation and remote communications do, nevertheless, underline the need to reappraise people's working environment.

These new patterns of working may mean that conventional space management is now inadequate. Spaces need to be created to define the new organisational parameters. Personnel mobility, changes in the space and time framework of activities, the partial delocalisation of workstations and jobs, make space management the key to strengthening links within the office and confirm it as the focus of social activity. This will mean rigorous planning to produce 'tailor-made' spaces which complement new methods of time and productivity management.

39

Office design should overcome any feeling of isolation where computers are used extensively

THE CHALLENGE OF
COMMUNICATION

The informative structure, which is geared to producing and processing data, is linked to the communicative process of relaying information. Communication is vital to a company's efficiency; it is essential for increased productivity and competitiveness in the market-place. What is now referred to as the 'quality approach' – the process of promoting a company's products and services, and the conditions in which they are carried out, rather than merely concentrating on the quantity of production – requires the efficient use of communication.

Since communication is crucial to a company's identity and business, it is present, in varying degrees, in all offices, although its application and demands may vary according to the business, its organisational structure, constraints and objectives. However, communication is used to ensure connections are made between various agents and data processing centres. Whether internal or external, the role of communication should not be neglected.

Internal communication answers an implicit or explicit demand for recognition which contributes to the meaning of an activity. A lack of communication can cause isolation and non-participation, leading to a deterioration in working conditions or morale and, eventually, productivity. Whether the interplay takes the form of team work, operational and planning meetings or an exchange of data between agents or departments, communication lies at the heart of the company's function.

The company may not only operate on this formal level internally. Close-quarter communication exists between colleagues and is usually flexible and not very structured: the use of support departments is an obvious example. The kind of informal and unpredictable exchange of information which used to be banned as an impediment to efficient productivity when employees worked under strict controls, is now encouraged in productivity patterns based on flexibility, co-ordination and co-operation: indeed, managements now realise that for people doing creative jobs, informal and incidental

Informal meetings – time well spent

meetings make a valuable contribution to individual performance. It is one reason why managers are encouraged to allocate space in such a way as to tempt people to linger in areas which promote this type of activity, such as cafeterias, reading and relaxation rooms.

External communication is used to reinforce a company's image and potential within its market-place. Whether or not it is carried out on a commercial basis to promote sales or services, it is the formative impression of the company's wealth of information. However, the creation of an effective corporate image for customers, whether actual or potential, requires the founding of contacts and communication and a well-designed reception and working environment. If a firm is trying to reach its customers, or promote its departments or negotiations/deals, its success or failure can be affected by the environment in which these operations take place.

The cellular office

By assessing a company's identity in terms of corporate image, management structure, work patterns and reliance on internal and external communication, decisions about the organisation of office space can be made more easily.

OFFICE PLANNING CONCEPTS

Over the years, four principal planning concepts have been established to define office layouts: the pool, the landscape, partitioned and semi-partitioned layouts. While they have passed in and out of vogue, and evolved from different attitudes to work organisation and efficiency, all are still present today to meet the needs of a company or a particular function. And emphasis on one style of organisation need not preclude the use of another. For example, partitioned rooms may be needed for conference facilities in a largely open-plan office.

The cellular office is the oldest concept, arising from the initial adaptation of housing to office use. It undoubtedly scores in providing acoustic insulation, visual privacy, and as a status symbol. Human contact is reduced, however, making the cellular approach undesirable in computerised offices, where contact is already diminished.

Removable partitions increase the flexibility, although cellular offices still use a lot of space.

The pool first made its appearance towards the end of the last century in the United States. Based on the Taylorian model of work organisation, it relates to the specialisation and distribution of tasks, and imposes the factory model on the introduction of typewriters and accounting machines. Rows of desks are arranged about a central passage, which allows quick glance control of the whole department. Efficient wherever simple and repetitive tasks had to be per-

formed, the pool also brought with it problems such as lack of privacy, and high sound levels.

The pool

Landscape offices were created much later, in the 1960s, by the Quickborner team, a consultancy founded in Germany by the Schnelle brothers. The principle was to improve the way in which tasks were carried out through easier communication and circulation of documents, enabling frequent interactions between work groups in more flexible layouts. To encourage more efficient communication, discrete working areas are not hermetically partitioned, but simply marked out. Each work team has its own area in which spaces are organised to allow paper circulation – the main information vector – from one workstation to another, without people having to move around and without disruption of the passage of information. Storing and filing equipment which is common to all members of the team is situated on the periphery of the areas.

However, in spite of certain unquestionable functional advantages, the landscape concept may lead to too great a density of staff, so that the original impression of an open, relaxed work space may fall foul of an untidy appearance with disparate fittings. Staff may also suffer from a lack of personal 'territory' and privacy and, as with pools, sound insulation treatment may be needed.

System layouts were devised to maintain the benefits of the landscape office, but eliminate its problems. The principle encapsulates the advantages of cellular and landscape offices, combining privacy with flexibility. By using fully-integrated system furniture, which combines panels of differing heights, easy communication can be achieved without sacrificing personal privacy.

When fully implemented, this type of layout with system furniture can become effectively a form of interior architecture, coping with considerations tra-

42

A successful landscape office

ditionally taken care of in the building fabric, such as wire management, lighting and space allocation. Considered from an urban viewpoint, it divides space to provide work and relaxation areas, with main and secondary circulation. Thus private and communication areas can co-exist within a fabric which, with independent furniture elements and a modular design, is flexible enough to meet both human and functional requirements. Such arrangements can provide highly economical use of space, with workstations covering 8 sq m (86 sq ft) to 10 sq m (107 sq ft), including circulation space. Once again, however, sound levels can be a problem.

However, a fifth approach to office design has evolved over the years – the combination office.

System layout

Combi (combination) offices. Efficiency and productivity depend in most offices on the type of space organisation and the quality of layout and fittings. While each of the four concepts has particular benefits, the most efficient and responsive office may often be achieved by using several styles, blending a mixture of approaches to respond to different office activities within the same company. A company's accountants may need cellular offices, while its secretarial staff may need to be together in a pool.

One element of the combi office

Indeed, by combining concepts a new combi-office design was developed in Scandinavia at the end of the 1960s, and has been further investigated by Harvard professors Philip Stone and Robert Luchetti. Grouping white-collar workers together, it provides a range of spaces which differentiate types of task undertaken. Each individual has a personal space for quiet work, occupying between 5 sq m (53 sq ft) and 12 sq m (129 sq ft).

The first combi-office, Stockholm 1979

Conference rooms

Rooms dedicated to specialist activities, eg, library and computer work

Cellular offices

44

These private offices are at the edge of a relaxed reception area. This space is also bordered by partitioned meeting and conference rooms on one side and dedicated space for library or concentrated computer activities on the other. In this way, all the different working disciplines maintain a close relationship with the reception space and the people coming into contact with the company.

Despite the simplistic convenience of these ideas, it is important to remember that any individual space solution should start with a look at a company's needs, constraints and objectives, which will be as unique as the space plan devised to meet them. The most suitable layout strategy may vary from one department to another within the same organisation, so the needs of the various groups of employees must be evaluated and met.

Space may be needed for formal meetings

SPACES FOR COMMUNICATION

Taking into account the facts discussed above, how can companies create spaces specifically for communication without ignoring the need for isolation and privacy?

There are still plenty of offices which have high-performance computer equipment, without adapting to modern working conditions. These offices fail, through landscaping, partitioning or semi-enclosure, to indicate what communication is about. Meetings are becoming an increasingly important element of office life and this change in work practice demands a new approach to space planning. There need to be areas for exchange of communication

and areas for quiet reflection; scope for groups and for individuals. There are various ways to deal with these needs; a combination of concentration 'cells' can be established within specific communication areas, where people meet for the duration of their co-operation. Such specialised areas may take different forms, depending on the type of business, from traditional conference rooms to more 'convivial' spaces. There may even be 'socialising corridors' which are well-defined from proper work areas. The kind of informal conversations that take place at the coffee machine or on the stairs still have a part to play in effective communication and provide human contact.

The design and planning of work areas must aim to generate good contacts between people and activities, in keeping with the existing or desired communications within the company. The size of working groups, the location of workstations, the need for visual and functional links between departments and agents, and the possible evolution of the firm's internal organisation and size of personnel must all be considered.

ADAPTABLE WORK SPACES

The rapid evolution of a challenging economy and increased competition mean that firms must be ready to change their organisation and office design as the need arises. The new space requirements of computer technology have produced a new generation of high-technology 'know-how sanctuaries' – 'intelligent buildings'. These offices have been designed to meet the challenge of integrating personal computers without introducing a mass of cables that obstruct everyday work. By the use of deep floor and ceiling voids, computer cables can be discreetly catered for; and office furniture with its own cable channelling can further improve wire management. It has already been noted that at present these 'intelligent buildings' are, to a large extent, theoretical. However, such pre-cabled buildings, which are likely to be the birthplace and playground of technological revolutions, are not the only 'intelligent' solution available for integrating modern equipment and optimising space. One alternative is high-wiring capacity buildings.

45

A majority (69%) of US white collar workers think the time they spend at meetings is 'normal', 17% think it is 'too great', and 13% 'insufficient'. The time spent each week by white collar workers at meetings also varies according to the size of the business: under 500 employees, the weekly average is 5 hours; over 5,000 employees, it is 6 hours.

Average number of hours per week: 5–6

Time spent at meetings per week

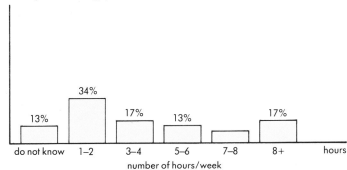

do not know	1–2	3–4	5–6	7–8	8+	hours
13%	34%	17%	13%		17%	

number of hours/week

Source: The Office Environment Index 1989 by the Louis Harris Institute for Steelcase.

46

Although these show great promise, they do not mean a company can avoid considering its own work space strategy; as their specifications become inevitably larger, the need for flexibility and forward planning/imagination will increase. Office planning will become a prerequisite for improved productivity, and providing for future needs will have to be properly managed.

Working areas will have to adapt to the structural and organisational evolution of the firm, as well as meeting any functional requirements. Successful office planning and design relies on a thorough appraisal of the structure of the departments, of work rhythms and methods implemented, and of the type and capacity of the equipment used. So a company must define its needs and strategy at every stage of its evolution. The planning will be efficient, flexible and well-adapted to the company only if it responds to forecasts of personnel growth, internal mobility, the size and composition of work teams, the nature of tasks to be performed and the hardware to be integrated.

The concept of flexibility has often been used as some sort of slogan to cover a vaguely perceived need. On the other hand, when treated in an undefined or excessive way, flexibility can have adverse effects; unconditional flexibility can produce uncalled for rigidity in some circumstances. A user's need to alter his workstation may conflict with a company's desire to maintain a coherent image; the moving of one workstation may mean shifting several others. However, if properly understood and applied with discernment, flexibility is still the best way to avoid obsolescence.

2   KEEPING TO A BUSINESS PLAN

To stay competitive, businesses need to maintain tight control of their economic equilibrium. The corporate headquarters and any costs related to its fitting out need to be assessed as part of an overall financial equation, and a life-cycle costing programme. Most importantly, managers should not be reluctant to allocate money to an organisation's building: as we have seen, it forms the first impression for the public and existing and potential staff, and, as such, should be considered a sound investment.

Any business plan needs to consider the performance that can be expected from the building. The management need to know roughly how much they are going to have to set aside for maintenance and cleaning, for example, and the cost implications of different types of spatial organisation. With careful assessment of the company's needs, and projected requirements, substantial savings can be made in many areas. Confronted by the options of new-build, refurbishment or fitting-out, for example, financial factors are at stake. Refurbishment projects can be subject to a VAT exemption clause, which can save thousands of pounds and give them the edge over other options.

In new-build programmes, variations in the cost of different construction methods – pitched roof versus flat roof, for example, steel frame or concrete – may significantly alter the final cost. Management also need to consider the return on their investment. While an enhanced standard of finishes may bring higher initial costs, such an outlay may increase the rental or resale value of the building. There are many cost permutations to be considered and the creation of a premises plan to operate in tandem with the main business programme should help to ensure that the company's money is well spent.

In analysing its budget, an office-based service company might expect to break down its costs as follows:

- personnel costs (salaries, benefits, expenses etc) – 75–90 per cent
- premises overheads (heating and lighting, maintenance, etc) – 6–10 per cent

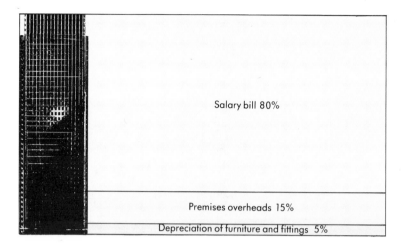

Salary bill 80%

Premises overheads 15%

Depreciation of furniture and fittings 5%

- building amortisation – 2–5 per cent
- depreciation of equipment (computer hardware, machinery, office fittings) – 2–10 per cent. This figure will vary depending on the type of business.

A well-designed workspace can therefore make a significant difference to a company's overheads by optimising human resources and floorspace, and helping to reduce running costs.

HUMAN RESOURCES

Not so long ago, increases in corporate productivity were measured in terms of investment in machinery and equipment. Man, as a production tool, was considered of little importance. As a result, the productivity of many processes has increased by more than 1,500 per cent this century, but growth in the service sector increased by 100 per cent in only a decade. In 1970 only one-third

Effects of reorganisation

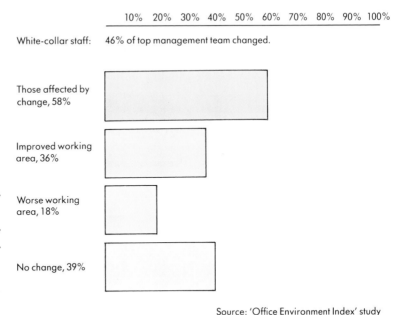

White-collar staff: 46% of top management team changed.

Those affected by change, 58%

Improved working area, 36%

Worse working area, 18%

No change, 39%

Source: 'Office Environment Index' study

49

Importance of the office environment

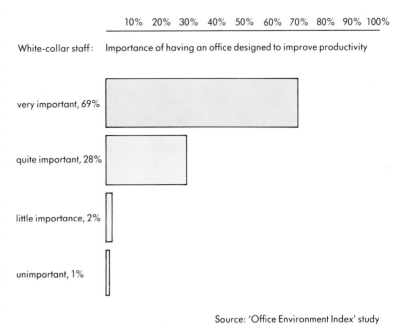

White-collar staff: Importance of having an office designed to improve productivity

very important, 69%

quite important, 28%

little importance, 2%

unimportant, 1%

Source: 'Office Environment Index' study

of the British workforce was employed in the service sector, but 10 years later the proportion had leapt to two-thirds.

Man is now recognised as being a company's raw material, and salaries have increased as a budget item by 2,000 per cent in Europe over recent decades to prove it. Optimising the use of human potential, by developing productivity, has become one of the fundamental objectives of sound corporate management policy. The Office Environment Index compiled by Louis Harris in 1989 showed that humans are more productive when they feel physically and psychologically comfortable; 80 per cent of respondents admitted to working more efficiently if they found their environment satisfactory. And if productivity is to be improved, the work space and equipment must be efficient in use. As a result, an investment in office furniture – which has a small impact on the overall corporate budget – can be more than counterbalanced by resulting increases in productivity.

This theory was proved dramatically in an experiment carried out by David Dressel and Joellen Francis in the United States between September 1982 and June 1984. Three similar administrative offices laid out in landscaped plan were selected for the experiment. Each catered for 17 staff: their average age was 44, average length of service was 12.5 years, and 67 per cent were women. Of the three groups, one was left in its original state, one was moved to a semi-open plan layout with existing furniture augmented by additional work and storage space, and the third was moved into semi-open offices laid out with new system furniture. All three groups were then equipped with computer terminals.

Questionnaires, surveys and interviews were used to review the progress of the three groups. Results showed that:

Control group (and original organisation of all the groups) – original conditions

- a move from landscape to semi-open layout resulted in a substantial increase in productivity and greater staff satisfaction;
- those given system furniture recorded a 20.6 per cent productivity increase, while those with existing furnishings and extra work and storage space improved by only 4 per cent.

Group 1 – existing furniture in new layout

The experiment concluded that not only would new furniture provide much higher levels of productivity and increased satisfaction, but the level of improvement allowed the investment in new furniture to pay for itself in just 11.5 months.

BUILDING COSTS

With the cost of office space now exceeding £500 per square metre (£50 per square foot) in London, and other provincial centres racing to meet that figure, no company can afford to neglect a review of its floorspace. This should start with an analysis

Group 2 – new office layout and new system furniture

of needs, looking at areas such as the topological approach to workstations, filing and storage capacity, the possibility of using vertical space, and the choice of an approach that is in harmony with the building, fittings and furniture. Space optimisation needs to be part of the business plan; office layouts should be reviewed so as to balance economical considerations with the most efficient allocation of space for the primary task of a company. The correct approach can avoid upheavals such as the moving of whole departments, and prevent the onset of unexpected building costs.

An effective approach to investment in furniture rather than buildings can sometimes bring with it attractive tax advantages. Before taking any expenditure decision, it is worth considering the full financial implications of an investment. By establishing at the outset the precise definition of any work undertaken on premises, certain tax savings can be made, and an organisation should ensure that its accountant is involved from the start.

Whatever a company spends, it will be liable to value added tax at the standard rate on any form of expenditure on furniture, fittings, and refurbishment works. Just as with other business costs that incur VAT, a business can pass on its VAT on its input costs to its customers as output VAT: most companies are able to do this, so long as the goods or services they are selling are liable to VAT.

For furniture, fixtures and fittings, it is accepted British practice that a company can write down on the reducing balance basis, 25 per cent per annum of the remaining cost of the equipment: thus for every

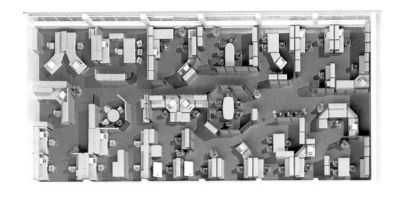

The number of members of staff who can be accommodated in open or system layout offices (above) is far greater than in cellular offices (below). It is worth considering, however, whether the economic gains in optimising space will be defeated by reduced privacy and personal comfort.

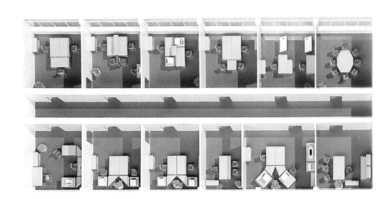

51

£100 invested, £25 is written off in the first year, and £19 (25 per cent of the £75 remaining) in year two. Using this method, approximately 90 per cent of the original investment is written off after 7 years.

Refurbishment costs remain a grey area, however, according to accountants Ernst & Young. If it is established that a cost is incurred in repairing something that already exists, then 100 per cent of the 'repair expenditure' can be offset against profit in that year. If the same item is thrown out, however, and replaced with new, then it is considered as capital expenditure and cannot be written off at once.

Complications do arise, however. The installation of double glazing, for instance, cannot be written off if it has replaced single-glazed windows, as that is not considered a repair. In some cases the UK tax authorities will allow a notional repair cost to be deducted where refurbishment takes place, but this is only by concession. It is important to establish the tax treatment of refurbishment expenditure to calculate the real net cost.

RUNNING COSTS

Effective office layout and design can provide substantial savings on overall running costs. Energy consultants Bernard & Company have established, for instance, that a well-designed building can, if also well regulated and run, consume 50 per cent of the energy used by an average office.

In addition, planning staff deployment and furniture investment effectively can have dramatic effects: 53 per cent of employees polled for the Louis Harris Office Environment Index survey had changed office within a previous 12-month period – at a unit cost of about £1,700. Such costs can be reduced by accurate evaluation of needs, and better management of the products required to meet those demands:

- a growth plan, giving estimates of future staff numbers, will facilitate effective space allocation and the optimisation of work stations. Such a study is costly, but neglecting to initiate one can prove more costly in the medium and long term;
- evaluation of floorspace use can reduce building expenditure;
- tighter controls on the furniture supply process, including stock control, can bring savings;
- use of standardised components will increase productivity, reduce inventory controls and cut overheads; and

- use of furniture offering wire management, can reduce the cost of electrical cable alterations.

It is also worth considering, particularly in volatile market conditions, the effect that interior design decisions can have on the residual value of a building. If premises have to be sub-let, or the company moves and has to assign its lease or sell a building, then an attractively fitted-out interior could add to the sale or transfer price, and could also improve the speed with which a new occupier is signed up. Conversely, taking a highly individualistic approach – using strong colours, for instance – might deter potential new tenants, who would have to contemplate the immediate extra cost of redecoration.

BUILDING ELEMENT LIFECYCLES

The building shell is the longest-lasting element and may endure 75 years or more. It includes major physical elements such as the structural frame, the building exterior envelope, and the vertical service and transportation (stairs and lifts) cores. The shell may see several changes of occupancy as well as changes of use. The extent to which it can respond to these changes is related to the services it contains.

Building services will usually have a life-span of between 5 and 25 years. At one time the mechanical and electrical specialists covered very nearly everything a user needed to know about building services. Now building services may well include air-conditioning, environmental control, power, data, telecommunications, information networks, and more sophisticated lighting for more demanding workers.

The shell is adapted to specific needs by means of finishes, partitions, raised floors, suspended ceilings, lighting fixtures, furniture and perhaps ducting and segregated trunking for power, data and telecommunications. These elements can have a life of only 5 years, and they are often extensively modified or even replaced on change of ownership or lease. This category, fitting out, can be subdivided to produce a fourth category, settings. These are elements that can be modified on a more short-term basis to respond to changes in the company.

Furnishings are no longer restricted to chairs and desks, but they include the full range of workplaces, cable-handling furniture, storage, acoustics and task (workstation) lighting. The description may cover demountable partitions. Furnishings have a short tax amortisation period (sometimes only 5 years) but the elements may last much longer.

---

3 SATISFYING PERSONAL NEEDS AND EXPECTATIONS

The third key challenge for any company considering change is to meet the demands and expectations of the people within an organisation and the people coming into contact with the group. In addition, any restructuring needs to satisfy the company's demands and expectations of those people.

Companies are under certain moral and statutory obligations laid down by employment, discrimination and health and safety legislation, but there are other more localised needs to be considered. Training of staff is expensive, so once recruits are found, it is essential to make sure they are happy with their environment, if they are to stay.

The decision-makers have to ensure that the spatial organisation they choose does not undermine company work practices. Cellular offices might be inappropriate, for example, in a broad-based firm which eschews the principle of hierarchy. Equally, it may be found that fairly junior staff need the quiet of a sealed office for particular tasks when private offices are perceived as a perk for company executives. Such dilemmas need to be tackled to satisfy people's needs.

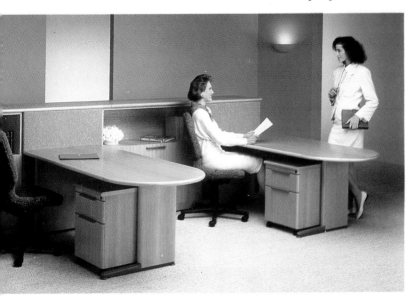

Pyramid of seniority and work organisation

Chief executive

Directors and managers

Specialist staff and technicians

Employees

External advisers

The traditional pyramid-type structure of business firms is being changed for a new model shown alongside.
This comparison clearly shows:

- the rise of outside assistance
- a sharp decrease in low-qualification administrative jobs. Thus at IBM, Descartes High-rise in Paris, the number of typists has sharply fallen, to be replaced by qualified secretaries, with a total of 80 for 2,800 employees
- an increase in the number of specialised managers and technicians
- a decrease in the number of managers, due to everyone's greater responsibilities
- the number of top executives is unchanged

54   In the past, management has had to tackle a set and limited régime of human requirements, in terms of remuneration and status, to maintain its workforce. More recently, however, demographic factors have upset even the few established hierarchical rules. On the one hand, the average age of the population in the West is increasing, while on the other the baby-boom generation, young, well-educated and motivated, are demanding more in terms of personal fulfilment. Because of their large numbers and the reduction in the number of top management jobs, promotions are more difficult and other forms of motivation have to be envisaged. So an upheaval in the system of values, the impact of a civilisation of leisure, and the resurgence of individualism have combined to promote a new attitude to work.

The allocation of space must be appropriate for each employee's needs

Today's workers seek not merely economic security, but also personal satisfaction. Increasingly, people are refusing the type of monotonous labour that fails to provide personal fulfilment, seeking instead a role in a living, participatory organisation, and a convivial working environment. They are prepared to commit their intelligence, knowledge and creativity, but in return they expect the company to show concern for them, and to be attentive to their work conditions. And while economics dictate that corporations cannot remove the threat of unemployment or banish all sense of job insecurity, they can at least provide attractive working conditions to motivate and keep their staff.

A survey carried out by Healey & Baker in 1989 showed tenants' order of priority for aspects of design within their buildings. They were: internal environment control and heating system; quality of internal finishes; the external appearance of the building; car parking; provision for cable trunking; condition of the entrance hall; toilet facilities; security; lift performance reliability and the arrangement for kitchen catering facilities.

Human contact at work is another ingredient of a good working environment, which is only now being fully appreciated. While new technology promises higher levels of communication and productivity, its use can actually reduce direct human contact – leading to withdrawal, isolation, and even inferior performance. Computer work is often abstract and stressful, with tasks being performed without much human contact: instead, the man-machine interface is the point of contact. The full physical and psychological effects of this work are not yet known, but there is no doubt that it often generates fatigue. The nervous tension caused by using a terminal, the effort of visual focusing, fear of not keeping up with technology and being just a small cog in a large machine, are the sort of negative responses such work can engender.

In the case of older employees who may find it harder to use new technology, maintaining a satisfying environment is more important. For those who express pleasure and delight in the use of computerised office equipment, the technology typically enhances their ability to do their job, serving as a powerful tool in their hands. For those who are unhappy with the technology, their jobs are often changed in undesirable ways and the computer seems to exert control over the work process, increasing their feelings of stress and anxiety. An appropriate working environment can, however, triumph over these problems.

Likewise, the growing number of women working in offices places an obligation to provide attractive working conditions.

Aside from career-minded women, recent research suggests that there are many who go to work for the human contact it can give them – and a good working environment helps to promote the social interaction such women seek.

All the evidence suggests that companies are increasingly realising that their main asset is their staff: senior decision-makers are consequently taking more interest in the working environment, and the development of internal communications, along with the appointment of increasing numbers of ergonomists and psychologists, bears this out. Work stimulation based purely on pay no longer meets people's demands, and a whole range of other incentives is taking its place – increased responsibilities, flexitime, shareholding, and assessment of group achievements all play their part. The provision of a working environment which motivates staff, and offers physical and psychological comfort, is an essential complement to this portfolio.

CREATING THE RIGHT PHYSICAL ENVIRONMENT

So what makes for a good working environment? Physical comfort is the first consideration, now covered by the umbrella of ergonomics and featuring factors such as seating comfort, lighting, the thermal and acoustic environment, and the colours and

55

materials used in the office. Ergonomics seeks to adapt the workplace to suit man. Based on an analysis of people at work, it attempts to identify the factors which will determine the physical and psychological comfort of the employee. To tackle these areas appropriately, a company has to consider its existing arrangements, number and type of employees, workstation layout and so on, before determining a correct solution.

Lighting: Inappropriate lighting will always generate visual fatigue in personnel, and can lead to more serious disorders. To achieve satisfactory lighting levels, there must be a balance of natural and artificial light, bearing in mind such factors as the location of windows, reflection from walls and other surfaces, levels of light required for various activities, and the type of artificial sources to be used. Consideration of lighting must deal with both the quantity and quality of light, to ensure that employees are not afflicted by problems of glare, dazzle and reflection.

Acoustics: Office workers are happy with sound levels if they do not exceed what is commonly considered appropriate, and afford the individual privacy, concentration and confidentiality. By contrast, an individual may waste up to 20 per cent of his energy trying to find relief from a noisy office. Measurement of sound considers its intensity and frequency, setting it against background levels of sound, and the reverberation properties of a particular space.

By considering sound sources – particularly those likely to create a nuisance – appropriate action can be taken to control them. This might mean the use of acoustic screens, absorbent equipment covers, deflectors, or other absorbent materials for room surfaces. Background noise must be considered, as it is vital to have an appropriate level: too much, and occupants experience discomfort and fatigue, too little and individual sounds such as talking may distract others unnecessarily.

Temperature: Whether an individual feels warm or cold in a room depends on a variety of factors as well as the actual air temperature. Air movement, warmth radiating from adjacent surfaces, humidity, the rate of fresh air ingress, and even clothing levels and physical activity all play their part.

Interaction between man and the ambient air takes place through convection – air moving past the skin or clothes drawing heat away. While draughts are undesirable, it is necessary to maintain a minimum level of air change in an enclosed space, to ensure that carbon dioxide and exhaled moisture do not build up, and to prevent the sensation of stale air.

Colours and materials: The décor of a work area, incorporating design, colours, materials and even works of art, is a fundamental element not only of the corporate image, but also for the well-being of staff.

Correct choice of colours and materials, in particular, contributes directly to creating a comfortable working atmosphere, which can be both restful and capable of generating activity: productivity will improve, while tension and fatigue can be decreased. Visual harmony is produced only by judicious selection of colours and co-ordinated materials. For those sceptical about the importance of such considerations, the colour of an office can even influence an indi-

vidual's blood pressure and pulse rate. Cold colours such as blues and greens relax and increase the perception of space, while warmer reds and yellows stimulate and invigorate, and limit space perception.

Are you sitting comfortably?

Seating: In the last century, many activities were still performed standing up. However, with industrialisation, and since the introduction of the first adding machines and typewriters, and more recently the computer terminal, most people are now seated for most or all of their working day.

The seated position is not, however, natural to man, particularly for the prolonged periods that are typical of office work – an average worker spends more than 1,500 hours a year seated. So in order to avoid physical and nervous fatigue, a seat must provide a high level of comfort, both static and dynamic.

The desk space – an individual's territory

Workspace as territory: To an employee, the space allocated to him is first of all a place where he lives, and an office, like any other area, is a territory. Within this he is boss, and he can set his space apart from others by such activities as decoration, rearrangement of furniture, and, sometimes, an attempt to reorganise the space so that it becomes either more ordered, or more disordered. These activities reveal the extent of an individual's freedom and capacity for control, and degree of autonomy, with the level of personalisation usually corresponding to hierarchical status. Some members of staff may ask for a certain sort of seating, or favour task lighting or individual control of a nearby heating unit, to regulate their own area. Changes also act as a message to others, pointing out aspects of personality, tastes, preference and habits. And while essentially this personalisation of the working environment is an individual activity, it also acts as a sort of ritual for integration into a group.

An individual may also seek to stretch or even reduce the physical space allocated to him, and by the same process various locations in an office become considered as good or bad, positive or negative, cold or warm, interesting or uninteresting.

59

PSYCHOLOGICAL COMFORT

Space allocated to an individual in an office has to be considered not just physically, but also in terms of the effect it has on that person, and the way he or she perceives it. Alongside formal physical boundaries exist personal territories or zones, which never correspond exactly to the actual limits of a place. An individual may appropriate and personalise this space, making a social and emotional 'investment' and helping to establish his status within the organisation.

60

carried out among two types of personnel (office workers and managers) showed the following differences: office workers' space is linked to allow a great number of contacts, while managers regard personal space as a place for isolation, helping concentration and preserving their autonomy and need for confidentiality.

These essential parameters of man's relationship to his work space are, of course, fundamental in office planning and design. It is important to note the essential difference between architecture and interior planning, as regards their respective impact on the behaviour patterns of an individual at work. Numerous observations and psychological studies have shown the small relationship between architecture and quality of work, but they have identified, on the other hand, a strong correlation between interior planning and design and work satisfaction. It is clear that spaces which meet individuals' needs

The need for privacy: Within an office, people often seek to establish a private domain – seen as a desire to protect against outside interference. Orientation, distance, size, the presence of partitions and type of materials all play a part in establishing the degree of privacy. Visual and acoustic screens, for instance, create real privacy, but may be considered by others as showing a desire to keep one's distance. Such conditions have important consequences in terms of discomfort and dissatisfaction: stress, for example, can be caused by visual and auditory disturbances, and frequent interruptions.

Privacy is generally a function of the degree of closeness and density of occupation, but different professional categories seem to employ different criteria for evaluating space. A survey

Panels aid privacy and reduce noise
transmission (left)

Low-level units maintain contact between
individuals

for appropriation and privacy are considered in a more positive way than rationalised, cold and mainly functional work spaces: each employee's human presence, personal markings, codes and values can be established in the former, but not in the latter. The location of the workstation, whether central or peripheral in the office, and other factors such as the type of partitioning, flexibility of furniture, and the extent of acoustic protection, all contribute to making office space humane. Such considerations can produce not just areas for working, but also for daily living, respectful of everyone's identity and

privacy, but without neglecting the need for conviviality.

More than ever, companies need the full support of their personnel if they are to improve their performance. And such support will be all the more genuine if people feel they can contribute to the decisions affecting their working environment. According to a recent study, almost 70 per cent of business leaders are in favour of greater staff participation in the planning of their work spaces. It is obvious that one of the key factors for successful office planning is the possibility of meeting would-be users' needs. It is also clear that such an initiative will

correspond to a growing desire on the part of individuals for active participation and the chance to take responsibility. In other words, employee collaboration will not only bring about greater efficiency – they will be the main users of such spaces – but also an attitude which will turn them into genuine partners fully involved in the company's success.

PART III

MANAGING OFFICE SPACE

Events have contrived to put office space at the heart of organisational vitality – and, in extreme cases, viability. Human expectations have risen, technological demands have imposed great pressures on the building form; and property and operating costs have escalated. In an era of heightened expectations and constraints, the modern office has certain clear objectives to achieve for the organisation it houses and of which it forms a key element.

It must, first and foremost, enable the organisation to perform its business function. If space is to help the organisation to function, it is clear that it must, operationally, economically and aesthetically, reflect corporate culture. And just as corporate culture and values constantly develop, the space that embodies those values and transmits them to the outside world must be sufficiently flexible to deal with an accelerating rate of change.

The modern office must play its part in the organisation's life according to the same economic rules as the rest of the business.

Premises decisions, like all other business decisions, must be related to standards, value and performance so that the premises plan – informed by the realisation that commercial buildings are assets, not overheads – forms part of the business strategy.

63

Formality and cosiness – the same approach to design need not prevail throughout

---

NEED FOR A STRUCTURED APPROACH

PROPERTY
Procurement
Jobbing works
Building contracts
Commercial leases
Relocation
Building insurance
Security

SERVICES
Energy
Information technology
Raised floors/suspended ceilings
Cable distribution routes
Telecommunications – BT v Mercury
Clean power
Air-conditioning
Air quality
Lighting

SPACE PLANNING/DESIGN
Designing for performance
Property record-keeping
Building performance (post-occupancy evaluation)
Occupational density

COSTS
Total occupancy costs
Total premises costs
Operating costs

MAINTENANCE
Maintenance of fabric
Maintenance of building services
Repairs
Cleaning

STANDARDS
British Standards
Fire safety
Space standards
Service standards

FURNITURE
Systems: cable handling, costs
Chairs
Visual display units
Ergonomics
Carpets

HUMAN FACTORS
Acoustics
Asbestos
Smoking
Health and safety

PRODUCTS
New building products – flat wiring; security glass; microporous paints; safety harness
New services – shared tenant services; computerised facilities; management bureaux
Copiers
PABXs
Partitioning

It must satisfy the human needs and expectations of people working within it or coming into contact with it, in parallel with satisfying the organisational needs and expectations of those people. And the office must meet certain statutory and moral obligations for the health, wealth and happiness of those people, taking into account the ways in which people in that organisation actually work and the ways in which optimally they could work.

Any comprehensive approach to meeting these challenges must consider the raw material associated with three key areas – the corporate values of the organisation itself, the human resources of the workforce, and the physical elements of the building. This is a vast body of material (above), encompassing topics that range from an organisation's main business concerns to marginal points of interest, and which, without a rigorous framework, could swamp the concerned manager.

Clearly this mass of material must be moulded to the organisational will. The group uniquely placed to address the fundamental problems presented by the modern office – the need to meet business, organisational, economic and human goals – is the facilities management team, able to use its skills to meet day-to-day, local, tactical ends without losing sight of longer-term, corporate needs.

1 BUILDINGS AND ORGANISATIONS

The relationship between buildings as physical structures and buildings as part of the business infrastructure, acknowledged since the 1950s, was brought into sharp focus in the mid-1970s by the extreme economic and operational pressures associated with the widespread introduction of information technology and the rising cost of building. For the first time, office buildings were subjected to the same managerial scrutiny as other means of production, and the importance of offices and office workers – sophisticated, predominantly white-collar employees – was acknowledged.

THE RISE OF THE FACILITIES MANAGER

Traditional building and office managers were unable to tackle the task of providing an intellectual, managerial or methodological framework for the modern office – demands created by the information technology explosion, heightened human expectations, and a shift in the world market from manufacturing to service industries. A new discipline, facilities management, emerged as the means by which traditionally reactive decision in this critical area could be supplanted by proactive, professional judgment.

THE FACILITIES MANAGEMENT TEAM

The challenge of facilities management lies in matching space and organisation – by getting the right building, or getting the building right – in order to allow the company to operate its prime business function more efficiently and economically. Achieving this match – marshalling often incompatible resources – requires the services of a team of people with a wide range of experience and expertise, which can audit, assess, cost and, if necessary, modify those resources. Techniques at its disposal include space planning; budgetary control; energy management; control of the corporate image through building, office, location, fitting-out elements, signage and logos; human resources management; and control of space ergonomics. Above all, the facilities management team seeks to create and manage the space, in the same way as any asset is managed.

The International Facility Management Association (IFMA), based in the United States, identifies nine areas of responsibility within the facilities management discipline – scoring in any two allows a manager to qualify for full membership of the association. The areas of work are: facility planning and design; facility construction and renovation; coordination of facility changes and relocation; procurement of furnishings, equipment and external services; development of corporate facilities policies; long-term facilities planning and analysis; building operations, maintenance and engineering; furnishing and equipment inventory management; and real estate procurement and disposal.

The make-up of the facilities management team will vary with the size and sophistication of the organisation, but its wide-ranging responsibilities indicate the fundamental truth about facilities management – it occupies a synoptic role, focusing the skills and points of view of architects and designers; building service, maintenance and structural engineers; quantity surveyors; building economists; user groups; information technology specialists; ergonomists; and management accountants. To deal with such dynamism, horizontal rather than vertical integration is required and the major players should be of similar status, advised and directed by the facilities manager and his team.

MONITORING TRENDS IN THE OFFICE ENVIRONMENT

The relationship between people and their work forms the basis of office environment studies carried out on an annual basis by American researchers Louis Harris & Associates and developed in conjunction with the Institute of Business Designers, and the International Facility Management Association. According to the 1989 survey, 90 per cent of top executives report some form of facilities management in their organisations. Sixty-three per cent view facilities management as a form of asset management, but only 51 per cent of facilities managers think their senior management would agree with that point of view. A significant minority (35 per cent) of top executives still see it as an expense and 44 per cent of facilities managers agree.

Nearly three-quarters of facilities managers claim that they have 'a great deal' or 'some' control over office automation installation, yet only 47 per cent of top executives think so. Top executives and facilities managers are, however, more closely aligned on their view of other

Decisions require teamwork

A Great Deal of Impact

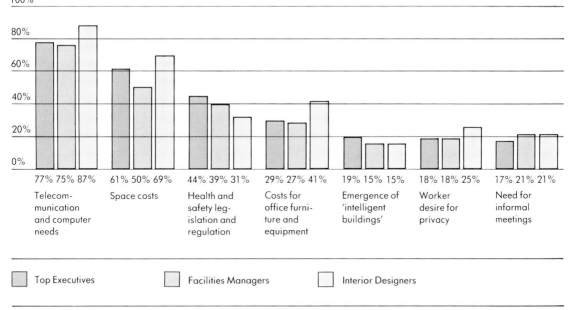

	77% 75% 87%	61% 50% 69%	44% 39% 31%	29% 27% 41%	19% 15% 15%	18% 18% 25%	17% 21% 21%
	Telecom-munication and computer needs	Space costs	Health and safety leg-islation and regulation	Costs for office furni-ture and equipment	Emergence of 'intelligent buildings'	Worker desire for privacy	Need for informal meetings

☐ Top Executives ☐ Facilities Managers ☐ Interior Designers

Source: 'Office Environment Index' study, carried out for Steelcase, USA by the Louis Harris Institute.

**Anticipated impact on facilities design –
5-year projection**

facilities management responsibilities. The same percentage of facilities managers and top executives who say they have a facilities management team in their organisation – 93 per cent – agree that the team's responsibilities include space planning, relocations and renovation of facilities. Long-range facilities planning is seen as the responsibility of facilities managers by the overwhelming majority of top executives and facilities managers (above).

Both groups identified telecommunication and computer needs as the key factor determining facilities design in the next five years, with space costs second; health and safety regulations third; cost of office furniture and equipment fourth; the emergence of the intelligent building fifth; employees' requirements for privacy sixth, and the need for informal meetings seventh. Compared to top executives and facilities managers, more interior designers selected the cost of furniture and equipment as having a great impact on facilities design, and fewer chose health and safety legislation (overleaf).

1989 OFFICE ENVIRONMENT INDEX FINDINGS

OFFICE ENVIRONMENT AND PRODUCTIVITY

Nearly 7 in 10 office workers surveyed felt that it was 'very important' to have the right kind of physical environment. Most of the employees surveyed identified the following features as 'very important' to productivity:

- proper lighting (92 per cent)
- comfortable heating and air-conditioning (81 per cent)
- a comfortable, adjustable chair (73 per cent)
- enough worksurface to spread out or display work (72 per cent)
- adequate storage and file space (65 per cent)
- sufficient privacy and quiet (59 per cent)
- attractive work area (57 per cent)
- office/work area close to colleagues worked with on a regular basis (56 per cent)
- appropriate arrangement of workspace and furniture (54 per cent)
- adequate meeting space near office/workspace (49 per cent)

COMPUTER USE

The overall percentage of office workers using a computer – 78 per cent – was the same as in 1988, but computer use had intensified.

PARTITIONED AND PRIVATE SPACE

'Partitioned' office space was the most common form of office layout. Office employees occupied a median of 50 per cent partitioned space, compared with 48 per cent in 1988. Surprisingly, 27 per cent of those who occupy private offices share them with someone. The demand for private offices has, however, fallen from 65 per cent in 1988 to 61 per cent in 1989, while the number of employees wanting open-plan layouts has risen from 11 to 14 per cent.

OFFICE STANDARDS

Only 51 per cent of employees said they had some choice of details of their workspace, furniture or accessories. However, a higher percentage of top executives and facilities managers said they had an influence on their working environment.

WORKPLACE HAZARDS

Workers questioned reported concern over a number of health hazards in the workplace. Eyestrain topped the list, with users of visual display units reporting the symptoms most frequently. Among those using a computer for more than five hours a day, nearly two in three reported eyestrain as a problem. Forty-nine per cent of heavy computer users considered radiation from visual display units to be a problem and 80 per cent felt that a comfortable chair is important. Only 24 per cent of those questioned said that information on safety practices for visual display units is provided.

More than a quarter of workers said that the quality of the air is a problem at their workstations, with the same percentage expressing great concern about radiation from units. Neither top management (22 per cent) nor facilities management (18 per cent) shared this anxiety.

EFFECTS OF MERGERS

Nearly half the workers questioned reported that their company had reorganised itself during the previous two years, with significant changes in senior management and operating procedures. Just over half of these workers claimed that the changes had affected them directly. The researchers say the findings indicate that the climate of restructuring, mergers and acquisition may contribute to an employee's mistrust of top management.

MANAGEMENT STYLE

A participatory management style is important to 59 per cent of workers. They also place priority on job 'participation' characteristics.

CANADIAN FINDINGS

Part of the survey was carried out among employees in Canadian organisations. Fewer workers reported that their organisations had health and safety policies than their counterparts in the United States. Air quality was reported by 42 per cent of Canadian workers as a possible work hazard, while only 27 per cent of workers in the United States cited this as an issue. However, this variance could be due to different smoking habits.

BUILDING PERFORMANCE

The Orbit report published in 1983 found that not only do organisations differ from one another, but they have different needs at various stages of their development. Facilities are therefore affected in two ways or, rather, in two dimensions – nature of change and nature of work.

Nature of change is measured by the frequency of relocation inside a building, or perhaps by changes in staffing. To deal with

The office may look good – but does it work well?

the change in size, a building should be capable of expansion, or subletting, and to accommodate staff changes, interior fittings must be adaptable. Nature of work is the extent to which operations are routine and predictable, or varied and unpredictable. The more non-routine the work, the more likely it is to need integration of different forms of expertise, more networking, more personal meetings.

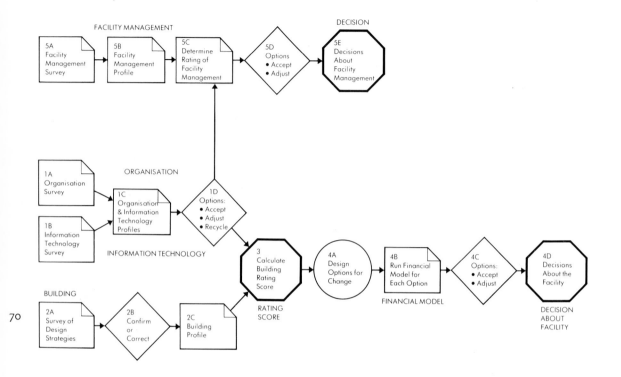

The Orbit-2 rating process

Although facilities managers spend a great deal of time informally assessing buildings – harnessing years of experience and expertise that alert them to ways in which new buildings should accommodate organisational needs – in the end, most judgments will be subjective, because objective assessments of building performance, measured against organisational needs, are still very new. The Orbit report provided an intellectual framework that raised the level of the whole debate, but it stopped short of providing independent judgments, empirical data and practical guidance. Orbit-2 made that step, introducing an explicit and comprehensive building rating process.

Orbit-2: The researchers drew up four surveys that would help a facilities manager rate a building in terms of the organisation that occupies it (above).

NINE KEY ORGANISATIONAL ISSUES

- **Change of total staff size** Is the total number of people to be accommodated in the organisation stable or changing?
- **Attract or retain workforce** How important is it for the organisation's success to ensure that highly qualified staff who are hard to replace feel satisfied enough not only to come but also to stay?
- **Communication of hierarchy, status and power** How important is it for people to recognise differences in rank, status, power within the organisation?
- **Relocation of staff** How frequently are people being physically relocated from one workplace location to another inside the office?
- **Maximising informal interaction** How important are informal and spontaneous interaction and face-to-face communication among staff?
- **Human factors in the ambient environment** How important to the organisation are the quality of lighting, air-conditioning, air quality, temperature, acoustics, etc?
- **Image to outside** How important is the image of the organisation which is presented to visitors from the outside?
- **Security to outside** How important is protection of information and other valuable objects from outsiders?
- **Security to inside** How important is the protection of information from insiders?

EIGHT KEY INFORMATION TECHNOLOGY ISSUES

- **Connecting equipment** How important is it that all or most electronic workstations are connected to networks, main frames, or other electronic equipment not located at the workstation?
- **Changing location of cables** How important is it to be able to make changes easily to the end points of cables that connect electronic equipment, whether at the workstation or in equipment rooms?
- **Environmentally demanding equipment** How important is it to meet special environmental requirements, such as for cooling, floor load capacity, humidity, dust, acoustics, vibration, static control, etc, due to the presence of information technology equipment?
- **Protecting hardware operations** How important is it for operations not to be interrupted, even for a few seconds; or for data to be protected against loss, delay, change or misrecording, due to problems with computer or related hardware – for example, due to interruption of electrical power, or other hazard?
- **Demand for power** How important is the need for primary and secondary electrical power capacity and feed, including vertical and horizontal on-floor distribution?
- **Relocating heat producing equipment** How important is it to be able to relocate heat producing information technology equipment to unpredictable locations within the office work areas?
- **Human factors; workstations** How important is the provision of suitable workstations, with ergonomically appropriate furniture, equipment and task illumination, and sufficient horizontal and vertical space for all required information technology equipment?
- **Telecommunication to or from outside** How dependent is the organisation on large volumes of uninterrupted telecommunications?

71

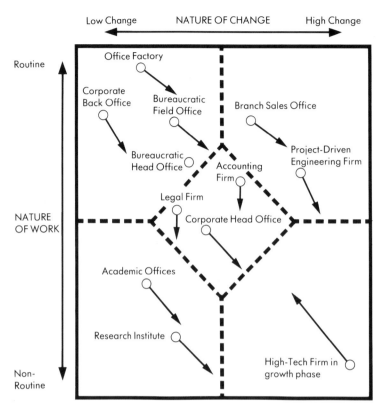

The pattern of demand seems to be shifting towards high-change, non-routine activity. This means that most buildings will need a major retrofit, since non-routine work seems to impose even greater stresses on a building than high-change working.

Source: 'Facilities' Vol. 3, No. 12 December 1985

MAPPING ORGANISATIONS ACCORDING TO THE WORK THEY DO

LOW-CHANGE, ROUTINE – accounting or administrative arm of a large company, or an office factory, with rows of people at computer terminals. Some small businesses in the service sector doing credit-checking, for example, or an expanding travel agency, could fit into this category.

LOW-CHANGE, NON-ROUTINE – research institute with highly-paid researchers.

MID-CHANGE, MID-ROUTINE – this would tend to be the headquarters of a mature organisation.

HIGH CHANGE, ROUTINE – project-based engineering company which takes on and loses people quickly as contracts begin and end.

HIGH CHANGE, NON-ROUTINE – a new high-tech company in its start-up curve, with high turnover of projects, operating under intense time constraints, organised with small teams of highly-motivated staff.

On the demand side, an organisation and an information technology survey identified 17 key facilities issues, which all organisations would have to come to terms with within 15 years (page 71). On the supply side, a survey of design strategies and a facilities management assessment describe the organisation and identify its position in one of five categories (above).

Having pinpointed a location on this map, an organisation should be able to assess the performance of its building in relation to the 17 key issues and establish what the most cost-effective actions will be in relation to its needs. The 17 issues will vary in importance both between organisations and within the same organisation at different times. For any particular issue, however, the building elements (above right) that will have to be modified to meet the company's specified needs can be easily identified (far right).

Building elements

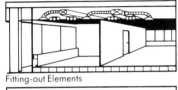

Fitting-out Elements

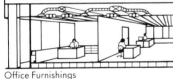

Office Furnishings

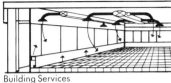

Building Shell

Building Services

The Orbit team warned in 1983 that certain buildings were becoming obsolescent – maximising savings on speculative office buildings had so reduced the longer-term utility of many 1960s buildings that it was cheaper to demolish them and start again than to refurbish. Architects had invested their emotional energy in the aesthetics of the design of building exteriors and interiors, but had neglected the ergonomic problems associated with office workers using visual display units for eight hours a day, or the need for the building to accommodate a high rate of staff changes and variable amounts of heat load. Developers had saved modest amounts of money in accommodating staff, but had lost much more in reducing the performance of the buildings.

Those predictions were quickly borne out by events. Organisations responded to information technology by producing new structures, using more specialists and less direct employment. Buildings responded by becoming more easily subdivided, more able to handle all sorts of electronic systems, better equipped with spaces for people, and having improved support services. The buildings that did not respond failed, not just as envelopes, but as a critical part of the business.

Large organisations are now convinced of this link between adaptability and survival, often preferring to commission new buildings with a project manager rather than an architect in charge. In the traditional, vertical design team, the services and structural engineers have no real chance of equality with the generalist architect. The operational stakes are now acknowledged by the more sophisticated companies to be too high to allow non-specialists in these areas to take overall control.

	Location & tenure (own or lease)	Building shell and form	Major building services	Local distribution of services	Fitting-out: Planning and design of typical floors	Office furniture
ORGANISATIONAL ISSUES						
1. Change of total staff size	●	●	●	○	○	○
2. Attract or retain workforce	●	●			●	○
3. Communication of hierarchy, status and power			●	○	●	●
4. Relocation of staff		○	●	●	●	●
5. Maximising informal interaction	●	●			●	●
6. Human factors: ambient environment			●	●	○	○
7. Image to outside	●	●			●	●
8. Security to outside	●	●	○		○	
9. Security to inside			○	○	●	
INFORMATION TECHNOLOGY ISSUES						
10. Connecting equipment			○	●	●	●
11. Changing location of cables			○	●	●	●
12. Environmentally demanding equipment		○	●	●	○	○
13. Protecting hardware operations			●	●		
14. Demand for power			●	●	○	
15. Relocating heat producing equipment		●	●	●	○	○
16. Human factors: workstations		○		●	○	●
17. Telecommunications to or from outside	●	○	●	●		

Building elements that resolve each issue

2 FACILITIES MANAGEMENT STRATEGIES

SPACE PLANNING METHODS

If the concept of facilities management is to do more than merely raise the consciousness of individual managers, it must prove its worth as a business tool.

Successful space planning must be founded on a precise understanding of the relationship between a specific organisation and its use of space, synthesising the total concerns of the organisation in a design methodology. A life-cycle diagram (below) illustrates the nature of those concerns, as the office planner contemplates all the factors involved in creating an office environment.

The need for change: In the first place, the status quo is being challenged, which is an important step for any organisation. The reasons for this must be established in terms of the company's characteristics, culture and growth potential as the quality of the eventual installation is dependent on the decisions taken at this stage.

The objectives in setting up a new installation must be clearly defined, taking account of the company's general method and field of operation, type of management and work patterns. An analysis of positive and negative elements of the existing installation will add further data to the case for change and help the project manager and chosen installer to produce a list of primary objectives. This could contain, for instance, the need to

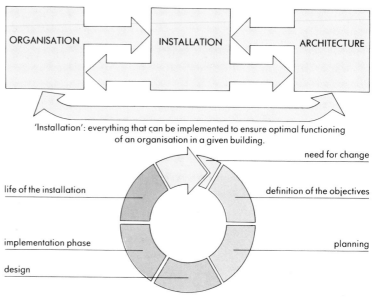

'Installation': everything that can be implemented to ensure optimal functioning of an organisation in a given building.

The life cycle of a tertiary installation

optimise existing surfaces; improve work conditions; implement new techniques; increase productivity; comply with the need for more operational flexibility; and make a greater contribution to the company's image.

Whatever the detailed components of the list, these objectives are critical to all subsequent stages – planning, design, implementation and life of the installation – and their feasibility should be gauged in the light of economic, functional and human factors.

Planning: Data must be collected and evaluated in four main areas: the physical aspects of the building; the needs and aspirations of individual workers; the collective needs of groups of workers; and the relationships which exist between groups of workers.

I BUILDING ASPECTS

- *Data:* structure and dimensions (width, depth, height, framework, floor loading); materials and finishes; plumbing; aspect and prospect; natural lighting; artificial lighting; characteristics and costs of temperature regulation; acoustic environment.
- *Evaluation:* specifications must be drawn up first as constraints, then as targets, and finally as principles and solutions. There are four main areas – partitions, lighting, acoustics, power distribution.

2 NEEDS OF INDIVIDUAL WORKERS

- *Data:* worktop area; storage and filing capacity; level of privacy and communication; necessity for meetings at workstations; signage.
- *Evaluation:* a manual of typical workstations (typology manual) contains, for each function, desirable characteristics of configuration, furniture components, application and ground area (footprint).

75

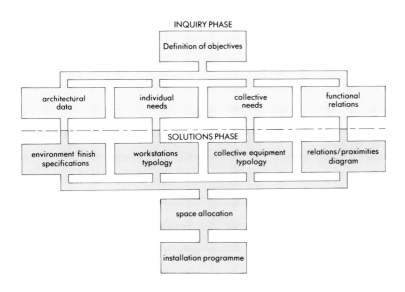

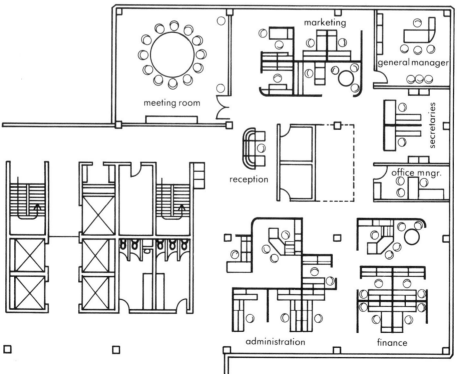

ZONING

meeting room

marketing

general manager

secretaries

reception

office manager

administration

finance

76

meeting room

marketing

general manager

secretaries

reception

office mngr.

administration

finance

After carrying out a zoning exercise (top) detailed furnishing layouts can be drawn up

3 COLLECTIVE NEEDS OF WORK GROUPS

- *Data:* special premises; meeting spaces; storage and filing capacity; equipment; furniture.
- *Evaluation:* assemble a catalogue of requirements.

4 RELATIONSHIPS BETWEEN GROUPS OF WORKERS

- *Data:* communication needs – independent of any building or workspace allocation constraints – between individuals, groups, services and departments, taking account of frequency, duration and urgency of such needs.
- *Evaluation:* draw up a diagram to illustrate the necessary relationships.

The area requirements dictated by the manual of typical workstations and the catalogue of group space needs provide the basic information for space allocation floor by floor. This operation is called zoning – the optimising of area and position for each operational unit.

The design of detailed pilot studies can begin only when the elements of the installation programme and, in particular, the typology and zoning layouts, have been accepted by the project manager. Perfecting workstation typology allows the defi-

nition or modification of each solution according to precise needs and constraints. Once the workstations are in position, the project manager can check whether everybody's needs have been met. Detailed final specifications can then create the required atmosphere by careful selection of colours, materials, fittings and furniture.

Implementation: The project manager checks that the details of the plan meet stated objectives, and hands over to the installer. The installation should be evaluated some time between one month and six months after the user has taken control, to check that the new office works as intended, and to provide additional data for subsequent projects.

Life-cycle: On completion, the installation enters a new life-cycle, linked to the management of its component parts. This is a vital stage for the organisation, since if carried out successfully it can substantially increase the life expectancy of the installation. Constant monitoring is essential, providing daily updating of all information on the personnel and the fittings. A standardised analytical system, based on the knowledge of users' satisfaction and records of personnel and equipment movements, allows for quick adaptation of the installation as needs dictate.

AUDITING SPACE

Organisations are seldom static; the political, economic and technical climate surrounding them is changing, which affects the technology they use to do their jobs, the markets they work in, the products they deal in and the activities they undertake. The result of this fluidity is a high turnover of personnel, shifts in the quality of staff employed, reorganisations of working groups and relationships and increased use of office automation.

In many organisations these dramatic changes have occurred piecemeal without a clear premises strategy. As a result there are uneven space standards, with gross overcrowding in areas; a changing distribution of activities to space, as the spatial demand for new activities and equipment is felt; inefficient use of space, due to ad hoc planning; disjointed relationships between parts of the company, and communication problems between buildings as annexes are taken over to meet unpredicted growth; deteriorating visual and climatic environment due to an increase in office automation equipment, and a proliferation of cables, noise and heat; and loss of financial control.

However, space audits allow the management to remind themselves of the opportunities and constraints of the building stock available, and review the 'premises policy'; reconsider the

BUILDING AND SPACE PLANNING DEFINITIONS

BUILDING DEFINITIONS

Critical floor area definitions used for measuring building shells:

GROSS EXTERNAL AREA (GEA): This is a term used by the Royal Institution of Chartered Surveyors which describes the office floor space as per the Town and Country Planning Act (1971). It is measured from the outside face of the external walls – that is the complete footprint on all floors.

GROSS INTERNAL AREA (GIA): This, too, is an RICS term. It describes the gross floor area which is the parameter for building costs. It is measured between the inside face of the outside walls and across all the circulation area voids and other non-office voids such as plant, toilets and enclosed car parks.

NET INTERNAL AREA (NIA): An RICS term referring to the gross internal building area less the building core area and any other common areas such as plant rooms, toilets, lift structure and lift voids. This equates with the letting agents' 'lettable floor area'. However, as lettable can be a negotiable term, the term internal area is used.

MAXIMUM USABLE AREA (MUA): This is the benchmark for comparing empty buildings and their space efficiency. It is measured as the net internal area less the minimum primary circulation.

MINIMUM PRIMARY CIRCULATION (MPC): This is the base minimum to satisfy the fire authorities. Typically, most cases would be covered by assuming routes 1.5m (5ft) wide, joining vertical cores and fire exits with no point further than 12m (39ft) from a primary route.

SPACE PLANNING DEFINITIONS

To assess the way that space may be most effectively used within the building shell, the space planner may use the following definitions:

DESIGNED USABLE AREA: This is the net internal area less the primary circulation routes as found – that is, designed primary circulation. Some judgment is often required in interpreting the boundaries of designed primary circulation.

DESIGNED OFFICE AREA: This is the net internal area excluding the designed primary circulation and the support area.

The designed office area is the term used to allow space planners to match the space required by an organisation (space budget) to the space available in a building. This can also be expressed as the sum of workplace and ancillary areas.

---

changing demands of the organisation in the light of greater usage of information technology; test actual use of space against an effective space budget and planning concept; and assess the effectiveness of the facilities management process in managing space and responding to change.

Definitions: The terminology developed inside a company has tended to conflict with the language used by quantity surveyors, letting agents, developers and planners. The building industry is concerned with the building shell as a container, while the space planner is concerned with the distribution of activities in the available usable space. The table above resolves the differences and provides a range of categories, from fixed properties of the building to varying factors which depend on the organisation's use of its premises.

An effective space budget should assess the requirement

Ground area definitions

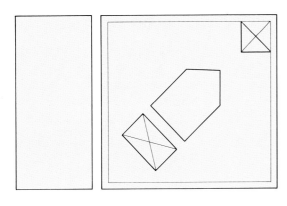

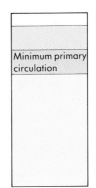 Minimum primary circulation

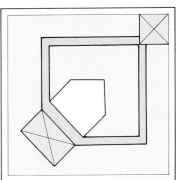

External walls

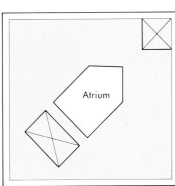 Atrium

Designed primary circulation

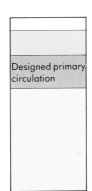

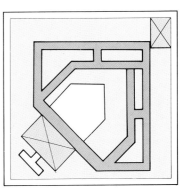

Core and structure

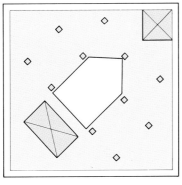

Designed primary circulation

Support

Auxiliary

Special

Workspaces

Ancillary

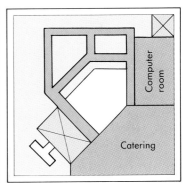

Computer room

Catering

Source: 'Facilities' Vol. 4, No. 2 February 1986

79

The workspace is the area given to each member of staff

for room in the workplace and space required for ancillary areas. *The workplace* is the space allocated to members of staff to undertake their job and it includes filing areas, meeting space, and any terminal desk space dedicated to the individual. This area may be closed or open-plan. *The ancillary area* is for activities required to support more than one workplace and this may include space shared, owned or managed by a group (such as group filing, terminals or meeting space). Again, this area can be enclosed as, for example, with a machine room, or open, perhaps for project space.

Secondary circulation refers to the route from primary circulation, between ancillary activities and workplaces. It is often included in workplace standards for ease of planning, but it is valuable to assess it discretely when measuring efficiency of space usage. *The support area* is the space needed for functions which support the operation of the whole or substantial parts of the building or organisation. It may be divided into auxiliary spaces which are essential for running the building, the goods area for example, and special spaces.

It may be useful to go by simple rules of thumb when establishing a space budget, indicating areas required for each member of office staff. This could be expressed according to several of the definitions above, but typically it is expressed either as designed office area for each member of staff (workplace plus ancillary and secondary circulation) or designed usable area for each employee (designed office area plus support). The average allocation for the workplace averages 7 sq m (75 sq ft) per person.

Building assessment: Common services such as heating, air-conditioning, window-cleaning and maintenance are all related to the gross amount of space and building volume, so that operating costs are sensitive to uneconomical gross building design. Developers have the most to lose from not getting the maximum lettable (net internal) floor space out of the gross area and they work hard to achieve efficient gross to net ratios. Sometimes their efforts are at the expense of lettable to usable ratios, which are the prime concern of the final user.

The workplace is the area given to each member of staff

The design must make adequate provision for cable management (right)

An assessment of the space available in a building should be compared with the following ratios as a benchmark:

- net internal area to gross internal areas of 70–87.5 per cent;
- usable to net internal area of 75–85 per cent; and
- usable to gross area of 55–70 per cent.

These proportions may vary dramatically depending on the number, depth and configuration of floors. The main reasons for the increasing proportion of non-lettable areas in larger buildings are the means of escape; the sizing of lifts and width of stairs; provision of toilets; the capacity of ducts; and the space for plant.

In practice, the amount of usable space to gross internal area may vary between buildings of similar size, a point which should not be taken for granted in building stock reviews.

Design features and use of space: The features which have the greatest bearing on the ability to use space effectively are:

- window mullions, ceiling grids and structural bays, which influence where partitions can be located and size of enclosed offices that can be provided;
- depth of building, dimension from wall to wall, location of cores and configuration of floor plan; the width of a

building may be too wide to provide for offices either side of a central corridor, and too narrow to accommodate enclosed offices, a workplace and a primary circulation route;

- the location of columns and service elements (HVAC units); and
- the frequency and location of power and data outlets.

For the most effective space planning, organisations should also assess a building shell in terms of its potential to accommodate enclosed offices; its adaptability for different styles of layout, and size of working groups; its capacity to accommodate cables; and the ability of its air-conditioning to cope with varying heat loads.

Organisations and buildings: How much space your company needs to carry out its functions is, or should be, determined by your business plan, with the guiding principles expressed in a premises policy statement. The premises policy may cover guidelines on the allocation of cellular offices, space standards and rules of thumb for support functions.

The space budget, or total amount of floor space needed, is the summation of the amount of space required for office space, support space, and expansion space. The space budget is built up by multiplying the number of staff by predetermined standards, and adding areas for support and expansion. Building shells, according to their configuration, depth and planning

81

grids, suggest planning principles to make the most effective use of the space provided. The constraints and opportunities of the building should be analysed in relation to the varying needs of the organisation. Does the organisation's current policy on the amount and quality of space per person apply itself efficiently to the building areas available? Could standards be varied to achieve the effective use of the building without impairing efficiency? Organisations which apply rigid space policies about size of offices, allocation of enclosure and access to views without considering the characteristics of the company may find themselves using space less and less effectively.

Carrying out the audit: An assessment of a company's use of space should:

- relate the amount of space the organisation is using to norms that may exist for firms in a similar business;
- consider the way space is being used in practice against organisational guidelines; and
- identify discrepancies of space provision and usage between parts of the company, people and groups of people. Space planning guidelines formulated by the organisation may bear little relation to changes in patterns of work and the technology used in some groups.

The quickest way to assess how effectively space is being used is a plan survey. This will reveal the proportion of space being used for circulation and support, and the amount used for people, which can be compared with company standards and expected practice; average workplace area per person in different departments; size and number of cellular offices.

With the help of building floor plans, a 'walk round' survey can be made of the building to discover the number of people in each room or area; the ratio between staff/VDU/peripheral (printer) in each space; the easily identifiable ancillary activities; and the rooms with specialist support functions. This survey should be done with someone from each department who can answer questions.

An assessment can then be made of variations in density and distribution of space usage from these marked plans. A more accurate analysis of space allocation may be undertaken as a building use survey for a major replan, as this will show how space is used and areas of wastage.

Finally, a furniture and equipment survey can be carried out to determine whether more or less furniture and equipment is being provided than is needed for the job, and whether the provision of shared furniture – such as meeting tables, filing cabinets and book shelves – is compatible with company

objectives. Such an assessment may be made by identifying areas of varying styles of work and then taking a 10 per cent sample. The survey may show actual patterns of space usage varying dramatically from planned standards, as in fast-growing organisations the distribution of space and demand may change as the planning process proceeds.

Ensuring effective space usage: The most effective evaluation is achieved when standards exist against which to measure performance. Effective monitoring may be undertaken against a planning concept, and workplace guidelines should be prepared when the organisation moves in. A planning concept will identify *capacity:* the number and size of individual areas it is possible to provide on each floor, and the total number of staff that could be accommodated using a minimum and maximum density; *zoning:* the most suitable areas to locate offices so as not to compromise the effective use of space; and *servicing:* a strategy for cable distribution and zoning of high-intensity cooling requirements.

Space standards are a necessary tool for optimising and managing the effective use of space. To ensure that standards are easily managed and economical to apply they should be:

- modular, so that partitions do not have to be moved continuously, but an intermediate partition can be installed in a large area to make two smaller units;

- in the minimum number of sizes (grades) to reduce arguments and minor adaptations;
- guidelines only, which can be adjusted to individual building configurations and grids, and reflect status, style of work and the need for privacy, or interaction.

Effective space management, good forward planning and procedures for monitoring space usage on the ground can result in significant cost savings.

Although identifying the appropriate building location, shape, size, building systems and furniture is necessary for the creation of a successful office building, it is not enough; the way in which the physical resources of the office are managed after initial occupancy is critical.

Are the right people getting the space they need?

83

PREMISES POLICY AND THE BUSINESS PLAN

The figure below shows the way in which the corporate plan will establish the need for premises to respond to the operational characteristics of the organisation.

The premises policy will be linked with two fundamental issues – the location and the performance of the premises. It must, by definition, be proactive and have the flexibility to cope with unforeseen changes. For example, the simple ploy of leasing more space than is currently needed and sub-letting on short-term leases (space banking) should avoid the need for an unscheduled extra move or split premises; it will also give the sub-tenant flexibility by creating a form of tenure not normally available on a head lease.

The performance criteria of the premises themselves (separate from location) will embrace, and should define, policy in terms of the quality of the internal environment, safety, comfort, image (internal and external), flexibility and adaptability, and economic operation (energy, service charge and so on). These two features – location and performance – will dictate the level of premises costs and a company's overall satisfaction with its building.

On top of the level of costs are the firm's policies of space allocation. Whether these are formal, informal or non-existent

space standards, the total cost of the premises is a direct product of the space and cost level. It should be possible to state the premises policy in terms which clearly describe the management's intentions for accommodating their present and likely future operational needs, and budgeting for them reasonably accurately. Even where, occasionally, there are alternative strategies held in contingency, these should be thought through, spelled out in full and thoroughly budgeted for.

It is highly desirable for the premises policy to be formally adopted as part of the corporate plan and this implies that it will be a written statement. Designated performance should also spell out the locational needs. The projected cost would be approved by the board and reviewed at least annually and immediately if changes are made to the corporate plan.

Strategic issues: The total costs are the product of performance requirements provided under the various cost centres of rent, rates, operating and fitting out. The term not only relates to the fabric, but it also applies to the overall performance of the premises component of the organisation.

The location is an element of performance which will accommodate organisational needs concerning availability of staff, accessibility to clients, pro-

Corporate business plan and premises costs

LOCATION	ORGANISATIONAL ISSUES	STOCK OF SPACE	COSTS	SPACE UTILISATION
Accessibility	Current size	Gross/lettable area	Rent/Mortgage	Flexibility
Single/Multiple	Projected size	Usable area	Rates	Space standards
Front/Back office	Type of staff	Configuration	Operating costs	Space planning
Efficiency	Functional groups	Condition	Fitting out	Density
Proximity to others	Patterns of work	Servicing	[Depreciation]	Support/Ancillary
In/Out of town		Availability		Information technology
Image				

Main components of taking stock

duct distribution and economics. It will also influence directly and significantly the level of rent and rates and the level of operating costs (including any service charge). Expenditure in buildings is linked to non-conformity and whether in a freehold or leasehold tenure, the cost of such distinctiveness will tend to find its way through to the annual rent or mortgage.

Many businesses try to set their premises costs to a level commensurate with the location. This will not always be the right strategy as the quality of the premises must be viewed primarily in the light of the business requirement, not just as a component of property asset valuation. Quantity of space is not simply a matter of space standards; the design of buildings affects the amount of useful space available. The configuration of the building shell, the position of the cores and column density, will all affect, to a greater or lesser extent, the ability of the building to respond to the operating imperatives of its occupant.

Taking stock: The key objective of this exercise is to examine all the facets of the quality, quantity and economics of the building stock to ensure that any attempt at optimising the use of the premises (for example by maximising energy efficiency) can be underpinned by a factual account of current occupation characteristics – that is, performance and cost.

Five major components of taking stock may be identified – location, organisational issues, stock of space, utilisation and costs (above). Consideration of each of these areas will contribute to an evaluation of whether the current premises are suitable for the company's corporate requirements.

Location: Companies often acquire space incrementally, growing out from a single building into a group of buildings in close proximity, as the size of the company dictates. The disbenefits are, of course, inefficiency through time spent travelling between buildings and duplication of some services.

85

Organisational issues: The relationship between the business plan and premises management is immediately apparent when staffing is considered. If a company undergoes expansion and needs more staff, it is important to know where the new staff will need to be accommodated.

Stock of space: The gross amount of space occupied by an organisation is, on its own, a poor indicator of the space available as it includes stairs, lifts, toilets and entrances. The lettable area has an obvious financial significance, and it is this figure which is most relevant to taking stock. The usable space in a building is defined as the gross floor area of a building less the core area and primary circulation. The ratio of the usable to gross area represents the efficiency of the building. A good, modern building will have a lettable/gross efficiency ratio in excess of 80 per cent and a usable/gross ratio of about 70 per cent.

The building services must be considered when taking stock, because their capacity to meet future needs will influence the suitability of existing space, and hence help shape the premises management strategy. The condition of the stock available has a critical bearing on its cost in terms of maintenance, repair and depreciation.

Space utilisation: As well as considering the physical attributes of the current space, taking stock should also consider the way in which the space is used. A simple calculation of total usable area divided by the number of staff will provide a useful occupation density figure.

Costs: The cost of the premises is the product of the price level and the quantity level. Finding out the cost of existing space – that is, without rents or mortgage, rates, operating costs, fitting out and (perhaps) depreciation – is a much more complicated task than it sounds. The main problems are lack of standardisation of cost analysis; costs are contained in a number of different 'pockets'; and difficulties in gaining knowledge of the actual contents of the cost centres. What the exercise does not provide, however, is a description of the performance of the stock as measured against requirements. The next stage, therefore, is to draw up a number of strategies based on a performance analysis. The strategies include: do nothing, with a 'business as usual' outcome; relocate to new premises; refurbish/upgrade existing stock to meet emerging requirements; or consolidate by refurbishing/upgrading some space while relinquishing/acquiring other areas.

Strategic options: The strategies to be considered depend on the nature of the underlying problems that have brought facilities issues to a head. These will include a shortage or over-supply of space; an inadequate internal environment; unsuitable image or location; a need for corporate centralisation or decentralisation; constraints imposed by premises and staffing costs; a need for greater flexibility; or property market factors.

Whatever the catalyst is, there are three generic options: stay and make alterations as necessary, move away to new location(s), or a combination of the two.

The decision to stay and make alterations may be dictated by economics, and probably means effecting some compromise. The extent and quality of the alterations together with any tenure factors will decide the economics of this option; sometimes, in the case of over-supply of space, part of the existing premises may be prepared for leasing or sub-leasing. The effect of making radical and expensive alterations to the leasehold property, for example, upgrading for information technology, must be carefully weighed in the context of the terms of the lease. It is not at all unusual for tenants to have their rents revised to a level reflecting the improvements they have paid for themselves.

There are other potential financial penalties to be paid in adapting an existing building, even an unused speculative development, to meet individual requirements. Up to 40 per cent of the cost of a re-fit can be spent on ripping out and/or altering what is put there by a developer or a former tenant. The temptation to optimise the real estate benefits is often very strong, but the purpose of the premises is to accommodate the corporate plan, so it is best to think of premises as plant to aid the business function and to consider moving to a new location.

Apart from the effect on premises costs the location(s) will have a big impact on turnover and availability of staff, corporate image and staff travel times. It is quite common for major decisions about location to be based on the personal convenience of the decision-makers and/or their spouses. The best way to expose such bad practice is to make a watertight financial case for the best strategy.

The performance of the premises against which the cost is assessed should be looked at under the following main headings: the efficiency of the design, layout and specification; comfort and convenience; image – external and internal public relations; flexibility; resilience; and capacity. Although it is not usual for these factors to be valued in monetary terms, they can be, within limits, to bring them into

Taking stock must consider how space is used

87

the financial equation and to consider the issue of value for money.

Frequently the existing building is retained as a 'flagship' in a compromise between moving and staying in the same location. In this case it is often best for the move to be well away – especially if the flagship is in a high-cost area – as staff who are moved out may take offence and leave.

Techniques of evaluation: There are many ways of looking at the costs of a premises strategy and for comparing one with another. These range from the simplistic 'annual premises costs' calculation to highly sophisticated techniques of cost benefit analysis.

Annual costs method: Here the costs are calculated for a given point in time (normally current) and a simple comparison made. This is normally on the basis of a 'first strike' process to aid discussion and to eliminate obvious non-starters.

Life-cycle cost analysis is a more sophisticated technique, normally involving a professional surveyor or building economist, who must attempt to forecast such things as the extent of rent reviews, changes in rates, premiums on leases surrendered, reactive and proactive maintenance, service charges and operating costs, fitting out, 'churn' alterations (an American expression relating to internal changes of numbers as distinct from the real ebb and flow of people into and out of the firm), and inflation.

The resulting cash flow projections will normally be discounted at a rate (or rates) indicated by the clients, who may wish to introduce certain additional quantifiable costs such as moving, replacement or redundancy payments.

PROPERTY RECORD KEEPING

Decisions on relocation, refurbishment or disposal of unwanted property may crop up at any time. If these questions are to be faced rationally, certain basic information must be immediately to hand and a comprehensive property record will provide the answer. Documents should be kept together, preferably in a fireproof cabinet and

updating should be on a regular basis if possible. A loose-leaf format is ideal as it allows for changes and additions.

It is advisable to keep accurate records of furniture

Location: Maps of the immediate area on a scale of 1:1250 will show the extent and nature of surrounding development, transport routes, services locations and development plans for the area. The local authority planning department keeps an updated record of plans for the area, so it is useful to keep in touch with them and have their contact names, addresses and phone numbers on file. Try to keep tabs on shifting local social and employment patterns, as this will help assessments of the market and local trends.

Ebb and flow of staff must be monitored

Age and history of building: It is important to know the date of construction, as this will immediately reveal whether or not the building complies with prevailing regulations, such as those governing fire safety. Try to find as many original architects' and engineers' drawings as possible. Modern custom-built properties will probably state within the terms of the contract that the client should be given a complete set of drawings for design and construction. Speculative buildings with tenants rarely offer such opportunities. Company histories, local libraries, local authorities and other sources are the best bet for information on older properties.

Size and type of building: Simple gross and net figures will convey a great deal. The gross floor area, as defined for town planning purposes, is the area within the measurements of the external walls, including the thickness of the walls. The net internal area, the rentable area, is defined by the Royal Institution of Chartered Surveyors as the area measured to the internal finish of the structural, internal or party walls, excluding toilets and bathrooms, lifts and staircases, plant rooms, common parts used for essential access, corridors where used in common or of a permanent, essential nature (such as for fire escapes), internal pillars and several other exclusions. This information should be kept in the form of regularly updated drawings and figures.

Estate agency information may be in square feet or square metres and will relate to gross rentable area. This will be relevant for strategic property decisions and comparisons. Architects' information will be in square metres for modern buildings, and can be measured accurately to give gross floor area or net rentable area. It should be available as part of the contract for new buildings, but can be found through local government planning or drainage departments for older properties when the architect can no longer be contacted. This is likely to be useful for all aspects of day-to-day management and any changes, such as extensions or demolitions and changes of partitions, should be recorded.

The number of staff working on each floor should be recorded, to maintain information about the area to occupant ratio. This is necessary for calculations of net floorspace per worker and workplace cost information. The regularity with which this material should be updated will depend on the extent to which numbers change. If the change is 10 per cent or more, it should be recorded, otherwise an annual assessment should suffice.

89

According to IFMA research, facilities managers face an annual churn rate of 25 per cent, but the level can be as high as 100 per cent in fully-occupied space.

The 'specification' of the building should be incorporated in a user manual, which is invaluable for relocation or major changes. These details will record the depth of space; plan form and location of cores; block form – plan and section; type and condition of services; structural type; how floors are serviced – from perimeter, floor, ceiling, central cores; and different use areas within the building – for example office, workshop, storage, loading, display.

Physical condition of building: A survey of the building fabric will need some professional input, but it is extremely important. The maintenance programme will be determined by the nature of the building and its condition, and structural defects must be recorded as soon as they appear, as the dates may be relevant in determining liability. A House of Lords judgment in 1982 redefined the starting point of the six-year liability period during which architects and designers would be liable for building defects.

Designers and contractors are a likely source of information, and previous owners may be forthcoming with specification details, equipment lists and maintenance records.

Using professional surveys: A schedule of dilapidations, carried out by an architect or surveyor, may form part of a contract. This can be invaluable, as it has to contain a lot of detail, sometimes even photographic, if it is to be attached to a lease as an agreed record of the condition. Energy surveys or audits are carried out by heating and ventilating engineers, while valuation surveys are carried out by valuers or chartered surveyors. These are, however, no substitute for structural surveys.

Barcoding: The ideal furniture inventory is a snapshot, an instant in time. As this is unrealistic, the data collection process can be accelerated considerably by using barcode systems.

3 SPACE ERGONOMICS

Ergonomics is the adaptation of the working environment for people's needs. As far as the office is concerned, this means ensuring physical and psychological comfort, by imposing standards of lighting, acoustics, temperature range, colour selection and seating.

LIGHTING

It is important to decide whether it is more appropriate to provide daylight by day and artificial light by night, or if daylight is inadequate to supplement it permanently by artificial light, or to use artificial light alone. Energy conservation and energy efficiency (solar gain/ heat loss) should be considered as well as the visual tasks being catered for. Other decisions need to be taken regarding the shapes of the spaces in relation to the size and position of the windows. Illuminance is the amount of light falling on to a surface, measured in lux (lumens per square metre) and the level required will depend on the type of task being performed (right).

GENERAL GUIDE TO TASK LIGHTING LEVELS

Executive and general offices – 500 lux

Typing and business machines – 750 lux

Filing rooms – 300 lux

Computer rooms – 500 lux

Drawing rooms – 500 lux (general); 750 lux (on drawing-board)

Industrial assembly areas – 500 lux (medium work); 1,000 lux (fine work, such as electronic assembly); 1,500 lux (very fine work)

Laboratories – 500–700 lux

Storage and circulation areas – 150 lux (at floor level)

Not only must task lighting be correct, but pleasant general lighting conditions must also be created (right). Glare can have a disabling effect or cause discomfort and the relative brightness of surrounding surfaces can be affected by reflection. The perceived colour of objects may change according to the type of light used, and its thermal message – warm, intermediate or cool – must also be borne in mind (far right).

BASIC LIGHTING SYSTEMS

General lighting – more or less regular arrangement of luminaries over ceiling areas to give uniform illuminance in space. This wastes energy in large spaces, but is flexible for workstation positioning.

Directional lighting – useful for display and combines with general lighting.

Localised lighting – ceiling-mounted. This is satisfactory if workstations are fixed.

Local lighting – supplements general lighting. This is extremely flexible if well-designed. This form of lighting is integrated into some furniture systems.

TYPES OF LAMP

Filament – has a warm appearance, but a short life and high running cost. It is often used for supplementary lighting, but seldom as the main source. Tungsten-halogen lights are more efficient than conventional type.

Tubular fluorescent – generally intermediate appearance, although warm and cool are both available. This is the type of lamp used most often in offices and laboratories. It has low brightness, high efficiency and comes in a wide range of sizes and colours, but flicker may be a problem.

High-pressured discharge lamps are available in several types including colour-corrected mercury, mercury halide, and high-pressure sodium.

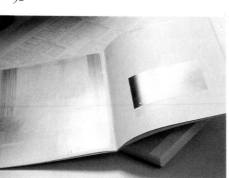

Lighting can help or hinder

Particular care must be taken with visual display units to avoid bright reflections falling on the task and indirect illumination systems such as uplighters are often the solution. Luminaires can be used to supply current, support the lamps, and dissipate heat, but their main role is to control the distribution of light from lamps. This is achieved by obstruction, using opaque enclosures with direct or indirect shading; by diffusion, using a translucent shade; or by reflection and refraction using a glass shade or plastic prism.

Natural lighting must also be controlled, especially in offices with computers, as its intensity can vary considerably with the seasons, the time of day and the number of hours of sunlight each day. External sunblinds can be employed to soften natural light and computer screens should be installed perpendicular to the direction of the light, to avoid dazzle.

ACOUSTICS

The acoustic environment must conform to certain criteria perceived by the user. For example, is the ambient noise level sufficient to provide confidentiality, without hindering conversation?

Intensity (or sound level) is measured in decibels (dB(A)). The audible range extends from the hearing threshold, 0dB(A), to the pain threshold, 130dB(A), and an intensity below 55dB(A) provides a comfortable sound environment in the office. Frequency, which is measured in Hertz (Hz), indicates the number of vibrations of air pressure per second and measures the pitch of a note. The human ear can perceive frequencies from 20 to 20,000 Hz.

Reverberation time must be adapted to the nature of the room, depending on its volume and the type of work being performed. Accepted reverberation varies from 0.6 seconds for an 8 square metre room, to 0.9 seconds for a 200 square metre room. In a closed area 80 per cent of sound is perceived by reverberation. Background noise is the continuous underlying noise of a particular room, made by air-conditioning, office equipment, street noise and so on.

Panels maintain acoustic privacy

93

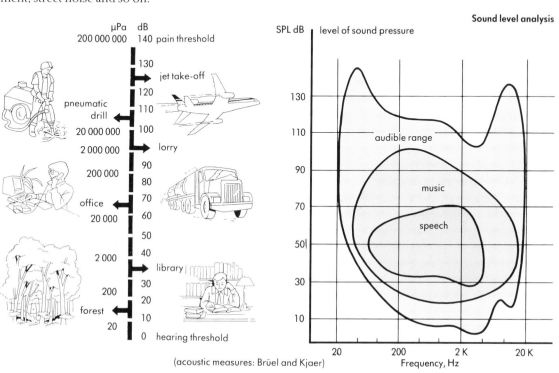

(acoustic measures: Brüel and Kjaer)

Noise level meter

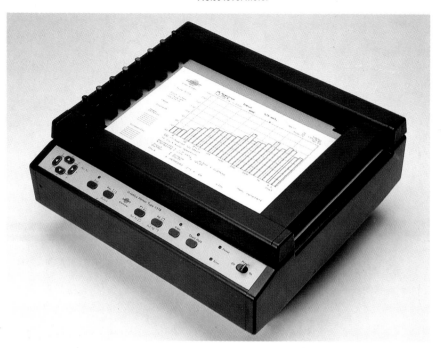

The sound level can be controlled by eliminating the noise (removing a piece of equipment); decreasing its intensity (reducing the volume of telephone buzzers); muffling it (putting acoustic covers on personal computer printers); deflecting it (with screens); and absorbing it with screens and false ceilings.

If the background noise is too high, the discomfort generates fatigue. If it is too low, peak noises such as conversation, equipment or footsteps can be startling and a 'white' background noise generator may be needed to provide a comfortable level of 45dB(A), covering normal conversation.

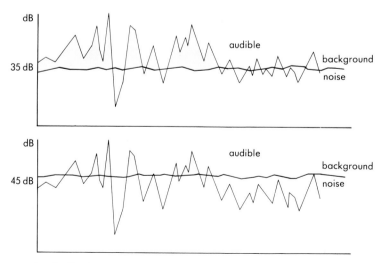

Levels of background noise

THERMAL ENVIRONMENT

Ventilation can be natural and the heating need not be part of a forced ventilation system. A forced system gives users the chance to control at least the temperature of the fresh air supply and, in the case of air-conditioning, the humidity. It will also filter the air to remove airborne dust and odours. If a forced fresh-air supply system is used (as opposed to natural ventilation or a simple mechanical extract system), this should be combined with space heating at least. If this system is combined with mechanical extraction, air can be recirculated in winter, for example, to speed up heating in the morning. During the summer, extracted air is exhausted

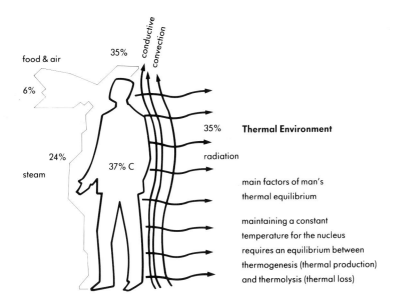

35% conductive convection

food & air **35%**

6%

steam **24%**

37% C

35%

radiation

Thermal Environment

main factors of man's
thermal equilibrium

maintaining a constant
temperature for the nucleus
requires an equilibrium between
thermogenesis (thermal production)
and thermolysis (thermal loss)

and only fresh air is delivered to the spaces.

Temperature is perceived physiologically, and is made up of air temperature, average temperature and air speed. Air humidity, rate of air renewal and nature of physical activity and clothing also play a part.

Air temperature (Ta) and average radiation temperature of walls (Tr): Thermal exchanges between the air and the individual take place by convection. Next to the skin, the air harnesses calories in proportion to the difference in temperature and flow speed. This temperature, often wrongly confused with the temperature actually perceived, cannot be separated from the temperature of wall radiation in perceptions of comfort.

In a space entirely covered by glass, with an inside air temperature of 20°C and an outside

temperature of 0°C, the temperature perceived by an occupant would be 9°C (if the average temperature of wall radiation is about 0°C). The 9°C corresponds to the resulting 'dry' temperature (Trs). This temperature, the mean of air temperatures and average wall radiation temperatures (Trs = 0.25 Ta + 0.55 Tr), provides a good approximation of an individual's feeling of comfort or discomfort.

For occupants to be comfortable, a winter temperature from 20 to 24°C, and a summer temperature from 23 to 26°C would be adequate. It is generally admitted that the difference between the average temperature of surface radiation and the average ambient air temperature should not exceed 3°C.

Air speed within a room influences the temperature as perceived by the occupants. For

example, an air temperature of 23°C, with air speed of 1.6 metres per second, will be perceived as 20°C with no air movement. In winter, average air speed in offices must be no greater than 0.15 metres per second. In summer, this speed can be increased to accelerate air flow on skin and clothing for more efficient cooling, but it must not exceed 0.25 metres per second, or users will perceive a draught. The location of the workstation must take into account the placing of the air inlet, where the air speed can measure 8 metres per second, and, for the same reasons, mechanical ventilation units must be readjusted if partitioning is moved.

95

Air humidity control is essential. Air outside at 0°C, nearing saturation point in steam (90 per cent of relative humidity), will produce, when heated by 20°C, air 25 per cent relative humidity when non-humidified. The air must never drop below the minimum level of 30 per cent, otherwise employees may suffer tract irritation due to dry respiratory mucous membranes, or smarting eyes, because of rapid tear evaporation. Too low a relative humidity can also cause static electricity spikes which are unpleasant for people and damaging to electronic data systems. To avoid this, the relative humidity of a heated room should be between 40 and 60 per cent.

Air renewal rate: The recommended air renewal rate in offices has been increased to 30 cubic metres per person each hour (40 when smoking is permitted) to allow efficient extraction of carbon dioxide, steam, smells, dust and pollutants. In facilities used intermittently, such as conference rooms, mechanical ventilation can be triggered by carbon dioxide or steam.

Physical activity and clothing: In the equation for calculating the predicted mean vote (PMV) of a large group of people subject to the same thermal atmosphere, the thermal resistance of clothing and the level of activity of its wearers are added to the parameters of air and radiation temperatures and air speed. This

gives a level of clothing/comfort temperature rating. Office activity of 1.2 met (on a scale ranging from 0.8 met at rest to 3 met in sustained activity) achieves a comfort temperature at 22°C for a level of clothing equal to 1 clo (1 clo is equal to winter indoor clothing, such as trousers, shirt and sweater). These mean vote methods also show the insignificance of factors such as food, age and gender in determining a pleasant thermal atmosphere.

COLOUR AND MATERIALS

These are fundamental elements in corporate image projection, both to visitors and employees. The choice of colours and materials contributes to a comfortable working environment

which can be restful, yet vital. The cold colours – blue, green and purple – are restful and increase space perception. The warm colours – red, orange, yellow – are stimulating, but restrict space perception. The brighter the colour, the greater its influence.

As a general rule, light and neutral colours, which increase light reflection, are better suited to offices, and allow for accent colour. Large areas of intense colours tend to cause weariness, or even rejection, and should be excluded. Light colours and pale shades provide a soft, luminous atmosphere, while pastel shades and middle greens create a soft, restful atmosphere, which is recommended for areas exposed to strong natural light. Monochrome (the use of tones of one colour) and shading (a group of colours with slight differences in tonality, lightness or saturation) both produce a harmonising effect.

In addition to these guidelines, some ergonomic rules should be applied: eliminate strong colours that could reflect on visual display screens; avoid dazzling colours on work surfaces, and aggressive colours, which generate irritability and loss of concentration; use colour to identify office areas; relate colour to activity type; and balance colour and temperature.

96

Restful or stimulating?

The management of materials such as lacquered finishes, glass and metal, will convey neatness and rigour; but wood and fabrics convey warmth. Try to use the same sensitivity when choosing materials as when selecting colours.

A host of professionals have worked for years to develop the ideal chair

SEATING POSITION

It is not natural for man to be seated, particularly for hours at a time, but the office worker will spend more than 1,500 hours a year in a chair. To avoid serious physical pain and fatigue, a seat must be statically and dynamically as comfortable as possible.

Multi-disciplinary teams made up of anatomists, orthopaedists, physiologists, sociologists and psychologists have drawn up precise criteria for work comfort. A databank now exists based on the response of the skeleton, muscles, tendons and intervertebral discs in a variety of postures. This has determined the extreme limits of seat dimensions – backrests, legs, bases, armrests – in height, width, depth, contour and mobility, and has also established the characteristics of adjustment, security and shock absorption.

97

The scientists found that:

- the inadequate shape and tilt of a seat's backrest could bring about the wrong position of the spine and create strong pressure on intervertebral discs;
- backrests that are too upright can hinder breathing;
- too soft a seat (and too hard a seat edge) can stiffen the posture and restrict blood circulation in the legs; and
- inadequate seat height causes bad blood circulation in the legs, poor positioning of the arms and stiffness in the shoulders.

Further ergonomical research has revealed the need for a 'dynamic' seat (following the concept of the 'dynamic seat position' proposed by Etienne Grandjean in the Zurich Symposium in 1968), which moves with the body through differential pivoting between the seat and backrest. These seats first appeared in Germany in 1976. They have three parts – a round seat, slightly tilted backwards; a flexible backrest, articulated by a lumbar section which provides adequate spine support; and a lockable pneumatic mechanism to regulate the backrest and seat tilt, allowing the seat to follow the user's movements.

Wolfgang Muller Deisig's Sensor in 1986 was an outstanding development of the idea. This was an office chair, designed to meet all office work needs – once adjusted to the user, the Sensor would follow every movement of the user's body, supporting every posture. The concept of dynamic comfort has continued to develop, in response to the new functional criteria imposed by computerised and multi-function workstations.

98

4 PHYSICAL RESOURCES – BUILDING ELEMENTS

THE BUILDING SHELL

Employment opportunities are shifting from manufacturing to service and office functions. The organisation of work is moving from large-scale manufacturing processes, consisting of firms with long production runs, to small-scale processes and short production runs, and a mixture of office, production, distribution and assembly functions in the same building. Market forces have made the expanding sectors of business rely on the application of very specialised and advanced knowledge and the harnessing of new technologies and, as a result, the balance of human effort has shifted away from straightforward production towards management. A healthy firm must constantly adapt its product or service to the needs of customers and to the latest technology. In order to provide this flexible response, many firms have become more integrated, with manufacturing, research, design, administration and sales located in the same building.

The increased speed of technological innovation has also meant that interior layouts must be able to change rapidly and easily. As a result many companies have abandoned custom-designed buildings with tailored interior layouts in favour of loosely fitting, ready-to-use shells with flexible interior components.

99

Starting from the inside out

Larger firms may be able to move into a purpose-designed building, but smaller firms may have to choose between a variety of buildings available for rent – new, speculative units; ready-made industrial or office stock built in the last 30 years or so; or redundant premises which are no longer suitable, or required, for their original function.

New buildings: Office space was until recently provided by developers who thought of 12m (40ft) to 13.5m (44ft) as being an optimum width, and a single occupant as the ideal tenant. Building space has become deeper, mechanical ventilation has become more common, and developers are now willing to provide a managed building in which the space may be leased by the floor.

Re-used space: During the late 1950s and 1960s the UK experienced a development boom and much of the stock available on the market at the moment is from this period. Many of the buildings tend to have insufficient floor-to-floor height for the installation of air-handling equipment; limited power outlets; and some have thin, glazed facades which suffer from solar gain, condensation in winter and poor heat insulation.

Building services: A typical building will probably have an average of four complete renewals of its services during its life. It is no longer acceptable, however, for companies to consider services as merely 'bolt on', secondary areas of concern and investment.

Few companies can afford purpose-designed offices

INFORMATION TECHNOLOGY

The impact of office automation on the office environment in the last five years has been incremental, and in retrospect dramatic. It has influenced the ergonomics of the workplace; the amount of worksurface required for personal screens, as well as the additional floorspace required to accommodate printers, and central processing units; the levels of lighting and the design of light fittings to reduce glare and reflection on screens. It has also determined the capacity of the building and furniture to cope with wires and cables; the need to extract heat from equipment; the need for acoustic barriers to reduce the clatter of machines; the pattern of work, and eventually the distribution of space; the desire for a visual language that can cope with the proliferation of equipment and cables; the cost of operating the building; and the cost of new building, refurbishment and fitting-out.

The potency of information technology and its effect on the modern office has produced a mythology, however:

- Technology can be dealt with once and for all. It can't; change accelerates, equipment is replaced, networks are adapted and offices are refitted.
- Information technology is for professionals only. It isn't; everyone will use it. Since information is power, tomorrow's managers will use information technology themselves, but most of today's managers will avoid using a keyboard.
- Electronic heat has been dealt with by low-power equipment. However, there will always be hot spots because of

increased penetration of terminals for the foreseeable future, along with printers, and lighting sources.
- Information technology saves time. In fact, it merely redirects it; the working day is increased to exploit the costly equipment, but people no longer have to be on the spot all the time.
- Paper will be eliminated. In fact, information technology increases paper production.
- Information technology saves space. People still need space for correspondence, documents and business discussions, and now they need space for electronic equipment, printers and printouts as well.
- Local area networks (LANs) will solve the cabling problem. In fact, for at least 5 to 10 years, most organisations will need more cables and connections.

POWER SUPPLY

To be flexible, electrical services systems, which may also include telecommunications, data processing and alarm installations, must allow outlets to be added or subtracted easily at any time. With the increased use of computers, visual display units and other electrically-operated equipment, it is important to provide sufficient outlets of different types in convenient positions. Trunking may also be

required into the centre of spaces, to provide for flexibility of layout.

Services require good access

FIRE PROTECTION

The local fire brigade should be approached for expert advice on appropriate provision for fire protection: make sure that not only is the right equipment bought, but that it is put in the right place. Check on appropriate fire prevention legislation, building regulations and requirements for means of escape and provision of firefighting equipment. Also check insurance requirements, and consider methods of detection and warning.

FITTING-OUT COMPONENTS

There may be some confusion between the concepts of fitting-out and refurbishment. Refurbishment is the process of bringing buildings into line with present-day needs. The term

finishes, or to adapt the environment, electrical and communication services to his needs.

The fitting-out budget should ideally contain only the following cost centres: internal divisions and doors; fittings; signs and graphics; and minor extensions and adaptation of services. Additional bills may, however, be run up on demolition and alterations; floor and ceiling finishes; and major extension and adaptation of services.

SHELL-RATED ELEMENTS such as partitions, raised floors and suspended ceilings can be dependent on fixing tolerances and the dimensional demands of the more traditional building trades.

Partitions are lightweight, non-loadbearing divisions which form secure, soundproof enclosures. They can also help work flow, provide privacy, eliminate distraction and act as a barrier. There are two types of partition:

embraces rehabilitation – the process of repairing and making good any defects in the fabric or services – and modernisation, which takes place at the same time and impinges on the design and specification of rehabilitated elements.

A building refurbished by a property developer will be left ready for fitting-out by the tenant. Nearly everyone in the property business, except estate agents, seems to agree that the standard of finishes and servicing which developers provide is quite unnecessary: the services may need modifying and the tenant may not like the floor and ceiling finishes. About 30 to 40 per cent of the cost of fitting-out new or refurbished space is spent on needless alteration works. As a result, there is a grey area between refurbishment and fitting-out, which depends on whether the tenant needs to provide floor and ceiling

those delivered to site in a number of small elements, and prefabricated, larger units. The first can be tailored to fit, but they are costly and difficult to demount and re-erect. However, since there is little evidence to suggest that in practice partitions are moved often, this may not matter. The factory-made systems come as large, modular panels, which are usually purpose-made and truly demountable. These qualify as loose furniture for the purposes of tax relief.

Raised floors were developed to deal with the special servicing needs of computer suites, and they usually provide the most effective, flexible and discreet solution for large networks of cable. Raised floors also allow more flexible use of space by eliminating the need for workstations to be near perimeter trunking. There are fewer unsightly, trailing cables and more flexibility for internal moves, although shallow raised floors do not give full accessibility.

There are two main types of raised floor – platform or jack supported (deep), and timber batten supported (shallow) floors. Shallow floors offer a service void of less than 100mm (4 inches) and are only suitable for cabling and some heating pipes. Deep raised floors can carry all services, dispensing with the ceiling as an additional service route. They can provide a plenum void and facilitate localised air-conditioning.

Raised floors lend themselves to fast-track construction techniques and provide a floor surface which is immediately ready without applying finishing screeds. They also encourage the use of uplighters, which are important in areas with visual display units, they provide localised maintenance of floor finishes and can even form a fire barrier.

Raised flooring can easily accommodate change

Suspended ceilings provide an effective solution where floor-to-ceiling heights are limited or where there is not a mass of cabling and it is not expected to grow dramatically. There are five types of suspended ceilings which provide varying degrees of concealment for services, an acoustic surface for absorbing or reflecting sound, and effective thermal insulation by sealing warm air into the required compartment. Suspended ceilings also provide a smoother reflective surface for uplighters than a solid, plasterboard ceiling and they can be laser-levelled, enabling better joining of partitions.

One of the disadvantages of a solid, traditional ceiling is that services have to be grouped together to provide specific, localised access panels; a fully or

partly accessible ceiling means more of the ceiling void can be used fully. Suspended ceilings can also act as fire barriers.

Solar control – external: Such features only control the effects of the sun, rather than the sun itself, but external shading or screening devices are the most effective way of protecting windows from solar radiation. There are several options available: external venetian blinds, with slats of aluminium or stainless steel, are adjustable from inside the building; vertical and horizontal fins and louvres may be fixed or adjustable, and of metal, asbestos cement or other materials; vertical screens may consist of small fixed louvres, mesh, eggcrate grille or perforated metal; and horizontal canopies may be solid or open (for example, egg-crate or louvre) construction. Finally, there are awnings which are usually retractable, with an aluminium framework and fabric covering.

INTERNAL SCENERY is installed independently within the building shell and supports specific activities.

Screens are lightweight, non-loadbearing, freestanding divisions which form barriers or enclose areas. Their construction is similar to partitions.

Floor finishes must be chosen bearing in mind that the floor may have to withstand abrasion and dirt, resist heavy tracking and static shock, and provide access to underfloor services. The quality of the sub-floor will affect the life and appearance of the covering but epoxy screed or end-grain woodblock often provides hardest wear. If the floor will be regularly wet or oily, specify non-slip finishes, as rubber and pvc can be particularly hazardous. If sound absorption is important within the room, soft floor finishes such as heavy carpets with underlay can help.

Epoxy finishes and vitrified ceramic tiles, bedded and jointed with chemical-resistant mortar, will provide the best solution in most cases where the floor is exposed to chemical contaminants. It is also important to remember that underfloor heating will affect finishes, and an anti-static finish can be used if static build-up is a nuisance, for example in a computer room. If people will be walking or standing on the floor for long periods, provide coverings with some resilience and consider the overall impression of hardness or warmth.

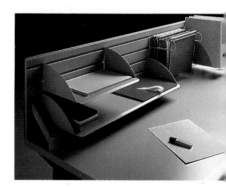

Finishes provide the interior 'feel'

Mezzanine floors are freestanding platforms, usually of structural steel, which may be used for storage, assembly, production, or offices. They provide additional floor space in areas with relatively large floor-to-ceiling heights and are self-supporting structures, as opposed to the platforms which form part of a multi-tier shelving system.

Security may be needed to protect against fire, flood, theft, vandalism or terrorism.

Furniture, fittings and accessories needs will change with time. Not everyone may think they need wire management now, but how many terminals might be needed in two years' time? Simi-

Durable flooring

larly, executives performing few, if any, machine-based tasks will still require storage space, and machine-intensive work still generates large quantities of paper. If frequent internal moves are realistically anticipated, standardised workplaces may be required to minimise disruption.

Space needs will expand and contract as organisations change and staff numbers fluctuate. For many, the actual worksurface area will be more important than the overall floor space, and selection of a system may be influenced by the need for formal or impromptu meetings around the workspace. The day-to-day space requirements of employees may well turn the space allocations associated with a traditional hierarchy on its head: support staff often need the most space, equipment and furniture, while managers and executives tend to spend most of their time out of the office or in internal meetings.

Increasingly users are getting involved in the design and selection of office furniture, as their participation is crucial if adequate provision of space for storage and accessories and ergonomic

design is to be ensured (above). Although full-scale mock-ups may not be feasible, a simple questionnaire can provide feedback and avoid expenditure on redundant items.

BRITISH STANDARDS RELATING TO FURNITURE

BS 5940: Design and Dimension (standard for testing basic ergonomic functions)

BS 5459: Performance (standard for testing stability and working components)

BS 6396: Safety (code of practice – no pass/fail certificate awarded)

Further information on British Standards relating to furniture can be obtained from the British Standards Institution (BSI) or the Furniture Industry Research Association (FIRA).

As one of the most critical performance criteria of modern furniture systems, the cable management capabilities of systems will feature prominently in most manufacturers' literature. Since cable management is relatively new, manufacturers seem to have favoured capacity at the expense of flexibility, neglecting to reconcile the rigid demands of services distribution with the changing nature of human functions.

105

Modern furniture systems accommodate cables fully

PART IV

HUMAN RESOURCES AND EXPECTATIONS

1 OPTIMISING HUMAN RESOURCES

One of the greatest opportunities for increasing the efficiency of an organisation lies in improving the human resource. More than a decade ago Likert, in his paper 'Human resource accounting: building and assessing productive organisations', maintained that benefits of between 20 and 40 per cent could be achieved, if management could be encouraged to channel their efforts. One of the problems, however, is finding some reliable means of diagnosing the health of the organisation.

A framework for this kind of diagnosis needs to cope with an internal environment which may be subject to change and evolution, but be capable of mirroring the subtleties of management style imposed on staff and their mode of working. Decision-makers may be faced with a whole spectrum of organisation structures and management styles, each making diverse demands and requiring different strategies.

Man: providing the greatest potential for efficiency improvements

ORGANISATIONAL AND MANAGEMENT MODEL

The methods used to diagnose the state of a company or division's health rely on two models, one representing organisational structure, the other management style. This concept was developed and applied by Lansley, Sadler and Webb in 1974 to analyse building and printing firms.

The models shown here are for the use of all those concerned with the design and management of buildings. They can be particularly useful to facilities managers for gaining an insight into the operation of their own departments and their interaction with the firm as a whole. The models have been used successfully by Liverpool Polytechnic's Building Performance Unit to analyse architectural and surveying practices, and in particular the maintenance management division of a large brewery.

The models are two-dimensional, with horizontal and vertical axes. Model A (above) focuses on the structural differences between organisations, with the vertical axis denoting the level of integration perceived and the horizontal axis the level of control. This produces four quadrants into which firms, divisions or sections can be fitted, depending on their rating. Names have been attributed to each quadrant according to the level of integration and control found to be present, so that they represent four types of organisation. Model B (right) shows four orientations, with categorisation of management style perceived according to combinations of task and people orientation.

HIGH INTEGRATION	
BUREAUCRATIC Represents a situation in which staff activity is prescribed by rules, procedures and written instructions. At the same time the structure is defined by a high level of integration, achieved by the use of effective communication of tasks and the creation of a sense of purpose by leaders **HIGH CONTROL**	**ORGANIC** A relatively high level of integration, achieved by freer communication, running both laterally and diagonally, through the organisation. Lower degree of control, with the impetus provided by self-motivated personnel, rather than regulation by rules and procedures
MECHANISTIC Emphasis on close control of staff activity, with limited integration, which means that each sub-unit is pursuing its own objectives and failing to relate them to those of the main unit of the firm	**ANARCHIC** A style which encourages staff to keep happy – with the hope that the results will take care of themselves

HIGH TASK	
HIGH TASK/LOW PEOPLE Staff are viewed in a similar context as other resources, to be used in the most rational and economic manner	**HIGH TASK/ HIGH PEOPLE** This implies a concern for achievement through subordinate involvement and teamwork
LOW TASK/LOW PEOPLE Defines the situation in which management appears passive and neither emphasises task nor people orientation	**HIGH PEOPLE** **LOW TASK/HIGH PEOPLE** A style which encourages staff to keep happy – with the hope that the results will take care of themselves

Model A – high integration

HIGH INTEGRATION	
BUREAUCRATIC • QS2	• Section A • Arch 2 ORGANIC • Section B • Arch 1
MECHANISTIC • QS1	ANARCHIC

HIGH
CONTROL

HIGH TASK	
HIGH TASK/LOW PEOPLE • QS1	HIGH TASK/HIGH PEOPLE • Arch 1
• Section A LOW TASK/LOW PEOPLE • Section B	• Arch 1 LOW TASK/HIGH PEOPLE • QS1

LOW
PEOPLE

Model B – high task

Data acquisition: To obtain the data needed to classify organisations according to the two models, structured questionnaires based on the format developed by Lansley are used. If the organisation or division is small, then the majority of staff are required to fill in the answers to 12 questions, each of which contains a list of options. Where the organisation is much larger, a stratified sample may be taken from staff drawn from each level of the hierarchy. A chart is also drawn up to indicate the formal relationships between staff, so that their perception of their positions can be checked against those of their peers.

Semi-structured interviews are also carried out to determine how consistent the answers are. The data is then analysed and collated to score an interviewee's perceptions of the components of the two models; this in turn provides figures on organisation structure factors, human performance and management style factors (all illustrated overleaf). Using these figures, firms can be categorised according to their organisation structure and management style, so that their place can be plotted in the relevant quadrants of the two models.

The results obtained from the three studies indicate the diverse structural forms and management styles adopted, some of which are not always compatible with the primary task of the firm. Although there is no single best way to organise a business or section of a firm, a strong body of research indicates that there should be some degree of congruency between the structure, the primary task being performed, and its level of uncertainty, diversity and complexity, if the organisation is to be relatively effective.

Results: The tables reproduced here show the scores obtained from a study of two sections of the brewery management division. The top table shows how both sections achieved above average scores for effective formal communication. However, their score for degree of control (the index of control intensity), was below average. Translated onto the structure diagram, this put the brewer in the organic quadrant.

The second figure shows the different scores for job and company satisfaction between each section. Section B scored below average for company satisfaction and Section A scored above the norm for job satisfaction. It was thought that this reversal was because B was isolated geographically from the main firm, while Section A shared a building with the parent organisation.

The scores for effectiveness of

	Effective lateral communication	Effective formal communication	Index value of control intensity x 1000	Structure category
SECTION A	40	53	480	ORGANIC
SECTION B	21	79	430	ORGANIC

Organisation structure factors

	Satisfaction measures		Effectiveness of organisational change		Effectiveness of communication channel			
	job satisfaction (1)	company satisfaction (2)	improved organisation effectiveness (3)	improved work atmosphere (4)	in picture (5)	job information (6)	few conflicting instructions (7)	willingness to listen (8)
SECTION A	40	50	40	0	60	20	100	20
SECTION B	66	38	14	0	38	25	50	50

Human performance measures

	People orientation		Task orientation		Managing style	External priority	Internal priority
	Perceived style	Morale priority	Willingness to listen	Diversion priority			
SECTION A	27.5	1	20	47	Low people Low task	13	33
SECTION B	26.25	10	50	5	Low people Low task	14	71

Management style factors

communication channels indicated in this diagram showed that staff in both sections had great difficulty obtaining sufficient information to carry out their jobs well. This suggested that existing systems were being used ineffectively. Coupled with this, the scores in row B indicated that superiors were unwilling to listen to staff suggestions for improvements. A particularly low score was shown for Section A. Factors affecting management style are shown in the third table, and these can be translated to give the position of the section within the management style quadrants in Model B.

Task orientation is largely determined by the extent to which superiors are perceived to be prepared to listen to ideas from subordinates and it is reinforced by the level of diversionary priority found to be present. This is reflected in conditions where senior staff are seen as competing with other divisions for resources or fighting overtly for positions of power.

People orientation is prescribed by staff's perception of the extent of decentralised decision-making and is reinforced by moral priorities such as considering the welfare of employees and the creation of a good working atmosphere.

Implications of results: The following strategies for achieving desired changes were revealed:

- The key measures of job and company satisfaction emphasise the need for stimulus through changes to the organisation structure. In the context of the two maintenance sections, this means a clearly defined career structure is delineated and attention paid to salary levels.
- Further attempts were made to restore status and morale by installing an enhanced staff training and development programme.
- There appeared to be a direct link between ease and difficulty of obtaining information for a job and job satisfaction. It was clear that the systems and procedures for communication needed to be standardised and simplified.
- Redesign of the organisation structure was needed to decentralise some of the tasks and responsibilities burdening senior staff. It was hoped this would give them more time to listen and implement ideas and to develop a more effective management style.
- The scores in the second table (columns 3 and 4) reveal the negative impact of previous organisational changes; a more consultative approach was deemed to be the solution.

Conclusions: The models provide a rapid method of diagnosis of the state of health of an organisation and provide pointers to those areas warranting further attention. If buildings are to be designed as effective environments in which to work, it is essential that the implications of the various structures and style are understood – as Orbit–2 showed.

2 ACHIEVING OFFICE QUALITY

Between 1983 and 1985 a team of researchers from Britain, the United States and Germany studied office quality, looking at the modern office not just as a physical product but in relation to the processes which go to create it. The office quality circle (below) summaries the general perspective used on office quality in the research. The inner circle identifies the different agents involved in office quality and the outer circle shows 11 criteria for assessing office quality. The theory is that office quality suffers through conflicts of interest between the different agents in terms of criteria. Investors and developers, for exam-

ple, are most interested in capital value and cost – the 'exchange value' – of buildings, while user groups are likely to be more concerned with 'use value' criteria such as adaptability and running costs. And even these criteria may seem less important to individual employees than 'habitability' – user comfort and control, and health and safety.

The report argued that, although it is impossible to specify physical absolutes for office quality, there are a number of universal principles which promote quality by resolving these conflicts of interest.

112

The office quality circle – agents involved in producing office quality, and the range of criteria for assessment.

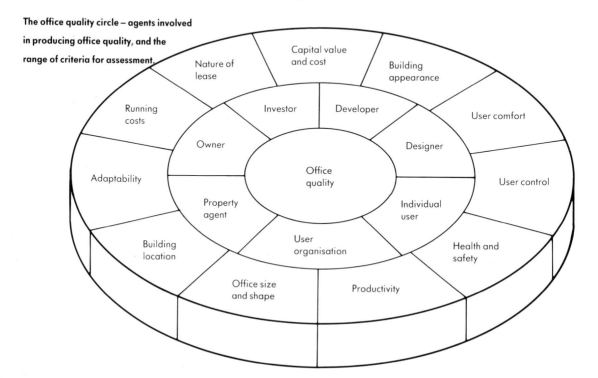

Source: 'Facilities' Vol. 4, No. 11 November 1988

Offices should be user–friendly

The office quality lessons to be learned from the comparison of office production processes in Germany, Britain and the United States may be looked at in relation to the three broad criteria already mentioned – habitability, corporate use value and exchange value.

Habitability: It might be expected that in Germany, where workers have a statutory right to be involved in decisions affecting their space, and far less speculative office building takes place, habitability would be higher. This is true in some respects, but in many larger German offices physical comfort needs were met while psychological needs for privacy, identity and control were undervalued or ignored.

Three factors contribute to habitability in German offices. First, a historically close involvement between the design profession and corporate users, combined with organisations' positive attitude to management science during the last 30 years, has produced a series of innovations in office planning ranging from 'bürolandschaft' to the 'group room' concept, and the 'office village'.

Secondly, the influence of the individual worker, through trade unions and other representative groups, has always been strong. Although unions, as in other countries, have tended to be-

come more preoccupied with keeping jobs rather than fighting for quality in working life, they have continued to produce influential reports. Thirdly, government has also been active in generating research and elaborating codes and standards.

In the United States the situation is very different. Office employees have no right to participate and unions have little or no power in the office. American workers patently have similar needs to their German counterparts, but they seem prepared to tolerate working conditions which repress or even undermine individual or group needs. The reason seems to lie in the power of the corporate value system and a general readiness to accept the often harsh plan-

113

ning and design disciplines this imposes. This situation contrasts markedly with Britain, where a certain anarchy prevails in many offices. Physical office quality is generally taken far less seriously and employers and staff often collude to create an atmosphere of domestic scruffiness in their workplace, which seems to have an appeal that the 'hygienic' office lacks.

Corporate use value: The aspect of office quality which seems to concern corporate users most is adaptability of the building to changing use requirements and, in particular, information technology demands. It is in the United States that the office production process has coped best with the problems of inflexible and unadaptable buildings. Three positive features of American practice can be singled out.

First, there is the separation of short-term building components such as services and fitting-out from longer term components of building shell and structure. These practices have now spread to Britain and, to a lesser extent, Germany, but they are less developed and effective in Europe. Furthermore, much office stock in Britain and Germany is still designed and constructed without the separation that allows easy replacement and renewal of interiors.

Secondly, leasing arrangements in the United States are more flexible than in Britain; standardised office space is

offered and let without fitting-out being done. Leases are also shorter and less restrictive on tenants. Thirdly, there is a wider range of fitting-out services, giving tenants greater scope for achieving and maintaining adaptable interiors.

Britain has a similar proportion of speculative office development to the United States, but these positive practices are far less evident. Germany, ironically, has not produced a stock

Users must be able to customise their own space

of offices with high corporate use value in spite of the greater proportion of owner-occupied, customised buildings and the close involvement of designers and management scientists. Many of these buildings have proved extremely hard to adapt to changing needs, and the reasons lie in over-customisation and the failure to separate short- and long-life components in the design.

Exchange value: The key factor here which would enhance office quality is the extension of ownership of the office to its users. Equity sharing arrangements and the availability of non-institutional capital for small-scale development would allow smaller organisations to take a proprietary interest in the offices they occupy or develop. The opportunity for the occupier to benefit from an enhancement of exchange value would encourage greater effort in creating offices of long-term quality. Britain has been particularly poor in this respect until recently, lacking either the condominium type of equity sharing found in the United States or the Depreciation Corporation type of investment opportunity available in Germany.

Key principles in achieving office quality: While some users know what they want and how to get it, particularly the larger corporate office users, smaller organisations tend to be more ignorant in the face of more and more complex office procurement. A tendency to undervalue the contribution of office quality to organisational effectiveness has a number of consequences; few resources are put into programming or brief preparation; managers of low calibre or little experience are assigned to project or facilities management; and little effort is put into seeking suitable premises or assessing the effect of unsuitable space on user comfort.

Users are gradually becoming more aware of office quality problems through the bitter experience of introducing advanced information technology.

They are asking more probing questions and making greater demands on their professional advisers, but there is still a long learning curve ahead and a dearth of appropriate information to guide them.

The key to achieving office quality in design and procurement is for the user to select the most appropriate type of service.

The proliferation of services in recent years has made this very difficult and there is no ideal solution. Some organisations will fare best with their own in-house expertise, while others need a principal adviser such as an architect to co-ordinate their efforts. Some others may achieve the best result through a package deal or 'turnkey' operation in

Achieving office quality is about more than just style

which the whole process is managed for them by one contractor.

Dwindling demand for office space in recent years has forced producers to pay more attention to user needs and the simultaneous arrival of advanced information technology has helped to focus attention on issues of quality. But will this situation last? A brisk increase in demand could prompt a return to old practices, although a residue of the accumulating knowledge about building quality could be expected to continue to affect new office development. The way to maintain the present trend towards office quality is to build up awareness and expertise among office consumers.

Feedback from use is a recurring theme in the discussion of office quality. It applies at two levels: feedback from the organisation using an office to the producer of that space; and feedback from individual users of an office to their management. The power of feedback depends largely on market conditions, as producers need take little notice of dissatisfied customers when demand is high. Enlightened managers have always sought feedback from their employees, but their views are more likely to be heard if staff are in short supply. The development of good evaluation techniques is crucial. Once producers and users have a ready means of

Trading rooms require a column-free space

measuring the performance of an office, regular feedback is more likely to be used to accumulate a body of knowledge about office quality.

Quality is clearly not an objective physical phenomenon as the same office may be loved by some employees and hated by others. Given that the basic functional requirements are met, the success of an office depends strongly on individual attitudes. Involvement of individual users in planning and management of the office not only taps an expertise which would otherwise be wasted, it serves to enlist people's co-operation and commitment.

Many of the large stock of speculatively developed offices in the UK proved unsuitable to the needs of their users from the first day and some have become totally unlettable. While poor design expertise was primarily responsible for these mismatch-

es, the buildings could also have benefited from closer consultation between producers and consumers. This could have been achieved in two ways: first, through forms of tenure which allow tenants to be brought into the development process earlier and to have more influence on it; and secondly, by making it easier for small organisations to finance and manage their own offices.

Adaptability to changes of use is becoming critical with rapidly evolving office technology, and although organisations and individuals have a greater capacity to mould themselves to ill-fitting offices than we give them credit for, the main contribution to adaptability must come from good physical design and planning. If a useful body of research knowledge is to be accumulated about good design, regular evaluation of offices in use will play a crucial part.

117

3 HEALTH AND SAFETY

Computers have brought new health concerns

New risks are emerging in offices that will inevitably force managers to take a more active role in health and safety issues. In addition, the advance of the electronic office is bringing fresh hazards to clerical work once considered absolutely safe.

In the UK the Health and Safety at Work Act (1974) applies to everyone except domestic workers in private employment, including employers, staff and the self-employed. It is concerned with the protection of people at work and the prevention of risks to the general public which may arise from occupational activities.

The Act's main provisions are to secure the health, safety and welfare of people at work, to control the acquisition, storage and use of highly flammable substances; to protect others against risks arising in the workplace; and to control the emission into the atmosphere of noxious or offensive substances.

Employers, employees and manufacturers, designers and suppliers are all bound by the legislation, which requires, among its provisions, that every employer prepares and issues a written statement outlining the organisation's policy on health and safety. It should include details of responsibility and accountability; committees and procedures; accident reporting and investigation methods; updating procedure; and sources of guidance.

RADIATION FROM VISUAL DISPLAY UNITS

These units emit low levels of radiation but a recent scare in North America suggested that they were responsible for an unusually high incidence of miscar-

STATIC ELECTRICITY

riages and birth defects among operators. Some organisations made all female operators of child-bearing age wear protective aprons as a result. However, the British Health & Safety Executive has concluded that there is no significant risk.

REMEDIES

- Advise pregnant employees to wear protective aprons or to stop working close to screens for the duration.

REPETITIVE STRAIN INJURY

This condition was described by an Australian occupational health consultant as 'the asbestos of the 1980s'. An avalanche of compensation claims is on the way there and more is beginning to be heard about the problem in Britain. RSI describes a family of injuries to the tendons, of which tenosynovitis is the most common, caused by excessive repetition of the same movement. Previously confined to industry, the condition now affects keyboard operators who work at consistently high keystroke frequencies. First symptoms are a

sore wrist or forearm, but in later stages there is acute pain, restricted movement and sometimes complete disablement. Occupational stress and poor working conditions undoubtedly contribute to the incidence of RSI.

REMEDIES

- Be aware of the problem, watch for any symptoms and act on medical advice immediately if they appear.
- Avoid jobs in which bonus payments depend on high levels of keystroking, wherever possible, as these encourage operators to work at excessive rates.
- Ensure that guidelines about maximum keystroking rates and work and relaxation periods are strictly adhered to.
- Follow ergonomic standards in the provision of adjustable visual display units and keyboard surfaces, chairs, lighting and so on.
- Involve people; the feeling that management is interested in the problem is likely to be the best course towards prevention rather than cure.

Static electricity can cause problems for people in offices and for computerised information. In some conditions walking across a carpet can generate up to 10,000 volts in seven seconds. Touching a conducting surface can then cause an electrical discharge with effects ranging from mild discomfort to a damaging shock. Static charges on computers can cause equipment to malfunction, magnetically stored data to be erased, and corruption of displays. A mere 500 volts can do harm, but the real danger begins at 3,000 volts. Static can be created by a lack of earthing, synthetic material, dust in the air, low humidity and high levels of electronic equipment.

REMEDIES

- Avoid synthetic materials in carpets, for example. Anti-static sprays can be used on materials.
- Ensure that all equipment is properly earthed.
- Use anti-static mats and earthed carpets near equipment.
- Check humidity levels and use humidifiers if the level drops below about 30 per cent.

119

- Ionisers may help reduce static build-up by maintaining a balance of positive and negative charges in the air.
- Avoid excessive dirt and dust in the air by filtering, if necessary.

FLUORESCENT LIGHTING

120 Researchers have suggested that up to one in three people working in offices and shops with fluorescent lighting is adversely affected. The hazards include headaches, eye irritations, skin disorders and even miscarriages. The problems appear to be connected with ultra-violet radiation from the fluorescent tube and the frequency of flicker of light produced by the tube. Canadian research has shown that such radiation can change the particles of air surrounding the tubes, affecting sensitive areas of skin such as that around the eyes. Ultra-violet emissions vary according to the type of phosphor used in the manufacture of the light tube, but flicker can cause headaches and may even trigger migraine attacks.

REMEDIES

- Pay more attention to selecting correct forms of lighting.
- Use thick, acrylic diffusers to reduce ultra-violet radiation.
- Install high-frequency control gear to eliminate flicker.
- Place light fittings with care to avoid direct glare into the eyes, or the positioning of a fluorescent light too close to the face.

IONISATION

Many people think that an imbalance of ions (electronically charged particles) in the air affects health. Science has not yet delivered convincing evidence of this, but that has not affected the sale of ionisers. Offices suffer from ion imbalances when negative ions get knocked out by metal air-conditioning ducts,

electronic equipment, man-made fibres and air pollutants such as tobacco smoke. All these items tend to acquire positive charges which neutralise ions, apparently causing headaches, nausea and lethargy.

REMEDIES

● If you think it will make you feel better, buy an ioniser, and it probably will. They do collect dust out of the air, relieving asthma sufferers, and they reduce the build-up of static electricity.

Most ionisers can be used like task lights at each workstation; they only need a power socket and cost less than £100. However, larger models are also available which can be mounted on walls or ceilings and incorporate fans to distribute the treated air. This type can cost about £1.50 per square metre (15p per square foot). Some ionisers can also be placed inside air-conditioning ducts.

NOISE

The 'hazard' noise exposure threshold of 90dB(A) over an eight-hour working day set by the Department of Employment's 1972 code of practice does not mean that all risk to hearing is eliminated at lower levels, but it was a sensible first step towards identifying a danger zone and drawing attention to a widespread industrial problem. Similar proposals and directives have subsequently been drawn up in many European countries, some of which deal specifically with noise levels for office workers.

Most offices will have noise levels well below the exposure threshold. Decollating and bursting rooms are an exception, however, as are rooms housing

items of equipment such as standby generators, frequency converters and chillers. Staff rarely have to spend much of their working day in such areas but, if for some reason this is necessary, they must be adequately warned, provided with ear protectors and, if possible, checked regularly with audiometry.

Attitudes are gradually changing as the psychological and physical effects of noise are being more fully researched and understood. The economic sense in preventing hearing damage rather than becoming liable for costly claims for occupational injury in the courts has long been recognised, and it is supported by standards, codes of practice and legislation.

121

PART V

CASE STUDIES

1   DUNN & CO

North Circular Road, London
Business: clothing retailer
Objective of installation: to facilitate a major corporate culture change, and improve operating efficiency
A total of 160 staff, of whom about one-third use visual display units, were moved into the new 1,850 sq m (19,920 sq ft) building in May 1990.
Layout: a mixture of open and cellular space.

CHALLENGES OF THE INSTALLATION

For the 1990s, Dunn & Co's management took a strategic decision to reposition the company to increase its market appeal; out went the dowdy, gentleman's outfitter image, and in came the contemporary men's retailer. While the public image of the company could be transformed by redesigning shops and changing the product range, it was realised that a change in corporate culture was vital to make a success of what the managing director described as 'a major repositioning exercise'. Staff had to be invigorated, involved in the break with the past, and shown that management were serious about their ideas.

124

Part of the break with tradition meant moving from the company's head office in Camden. Occupied by Dunn's since its foundation early this century, the offices were arranged on seven levels, with cellular spaces, featuring a mixture of old and new furniture in all types and sizes.

SOLUTION

Dunn's chose to occupy a speculative building, newly completed and offering an appropriate mix of office and warehouse space. Office space on three levels was provided prefinished with underfloor service trunking, carpeting and a false ceiling containing diffuse lighting. The company chose to remove one-third of the lighting, while other finishes were retained. Windows at the perimeter of the offices could all be opened as required.

To furnish the offices, the company chose to offer staff a wide choice of options, but based around a simple formula. One range of furniture was selected to be used throughout, as were task lights, and uplighters; apart from normal considerations of functional efficiency and cost, the choice was largely based on creating the right 'look' in the office, emphasising the fashion feel of Dunn's new corporate culture. Everyone was to have the same colour and finishes – a combination of calming blues and greys which were selected to match the building fabric. The conscious standard treatment for all removed any staff-management divide, and emphasised the importance of every individual to the organisation.

Staff were then allowed to choose their own layout of workstation, and their own mix of lighting. Working relationships with others were already established from the pre-vious office so, although space planners were used to guide lay-outs, staff on occasion disagreed and organised their own layouts. Management fully approved of this, following the argument that those who had to work in the offices could probably figure out what would make them com-fortable. Besides, the decentral-ised attitude of personal respon-sibility and choice fitted with the

new corporate culture. Space in the new premises was not at a premium, so generous allocations for each member of staff could be tried.

While much of the office is open plan, on the basis of work units, staff could request cellular offices on the ground of confidentiality and these were created using glazed partitions. Four weeks on from the installation, staff were invited to select plants and pictures to customise their workspaces.

By giving staff the choice, the company has noticed an incredible change in their attitude, with a sustainable improvement in productivity of between 25 and 30 per cent. With such an organic approach to the office layout, there have been teething problems: some staff preferred being told how to arrange their workplace, almost scared of the choices presented to them, while another group, who spread out in the space available, subsequently shuffled their desks closer together, apeing the arrangement of their previous offices, in which they had felt comfortable. The approach, and choice of furniture system, however, allowed this to take place; staff were able to achieve a comfortable working environment, without disrupting the company's business efficiency as they tried out the options available to them.

2   BURMAH CASTROL

Swindon, Wiltshire
Business: oil company
Objective of installation: to convert an office from cellular to open plan, with the aim of improving team interaction and coping with an increase in the use of computers
A total of about 75 staff were involved, with up to 90 per cent using visual display units, on a 1,950sq m (21,000sq ft) floor, of which 185sq m (2,000sq ft) is occupied by a library. The installation was carried out in early 1990.
Layout: predominantly open plan, with 24 cellular offices.

CHALLENGES OF THE INSTALLATION

Burmah Castrol completed the integration of the two halves of its business in mid-1990. The period leading up to this involved a reconsideration of the company's profile, and its space requirements.

The company occupied a building constructed in 1972 that placed constraints on space planning, as it had an inflexible core and little provision for the increasing use of computers. It wanted to upgrade its offices to improve its profile and to reflect a change in management style that called for more interaction and better communication. In the existing layout, cellular offices around the building's perimeter restricted the effectiveness of the building's air-conditioning, and limited natural light levels in a central open-plan area. Staff were to be involved at all levels of the changes.

SOLUTION

The department was refurbished in phases, moving staff as the work progressed. Departments were grouped as before, but they were organised so that they could share facilities such as printers, meeting areas, storage and supervisory workstations. Management offices, previously arranged around the building's perimeter, were moved to the core to provide better interaction with the various teams and to improve the performance of the building's air supply system.

The management wanted to create an efficient working environment to cope with the demands of the increasing number of visual display units, without sacrificing a traditional atmosphere in the office. Staff showed a marked preference for wood-based finishes, so as a result, a traditional-looking furniture system was selected, with full

129

technical facilities to accommodate computers and associated cables. Executives occupying cellular offices were given a choice of three ranges of furniture, all in keeping with the overall feel of the installation.

High and medium level screening was used to differentiate between departments, and to emphasise status and personal storage areas. In this way, the employees' need for privacy was met, without undermining the open-plan layout. Large areas of glass were used to define cellular offices, avoiding previous problems of dark corridors, and underlining Burmah's intention to improve openness and communication between staff in the new layout. Ambient downlighting was used to improve lighting levels in the building.

Some initial problems were posed by the need for bulk storage during the reorganisation of the finance department, for example. This was solved by providing central banks of filing, softened by the use of fabric, supplemented by strategic elements for predetermined tasks carried out within the work groups.

Due to the involvement of staff at every stage of the changes, the resulting environment was deemed to be successful in terms of appearance, functionality and budget. The reaction of staff has been positive, after the initial shock of the dramatic change in working environment.

3 CITIBANK

London, England
Business: banking
Objective of installation: motivate staff
by providing physical and psychological
comfort
An office of 2,000sq m (21,530sq ft)
was fitted out in 1988 for 150 staff, all
users of computer terminals. Lighting
was provided by general and task lights.
Layout: 70 per cent cellular, 30 per cent
open.

CHALLENGES OF THE INSTALLATION

Citibank's corporate finance division occupied several offices around London, which were to be grouped together in a new office at London Bridge City, a new development on the south bank of the Thames. While many of the staff were to move only about 3.5 km (2 miles), there was widespread prejudice against working on the 'south bank', and some tension was evident between the different people who were to be brought together in the new building.

Citibank had taken space on the fifth floor of the Cottons Building at London Bridge City for the new office. Wrapped in a U-shape around a large entrance atrium, much of the space looked into the atrium or across the Thames. The specification issued to space planners required the solution to accommodate frequent changes, allowing mobility of personnel, while allowing for a high percentage of cellular offices and conference rooms. However, the offices also

had to be convivial, warm and pleasant to work in.

SOLUTION

Any plan had to make the most of the building's proximity to the river, while still maximising flexibility and ensuring the appropriate density of occupation. Most of the offices were

therefore spread out around the atrium, with a combination of closed and open spaces. This arrangement made the most of the brightness provided by the glazed atrium walls, while glazed partitions allowed light to penetrate deep into the office. One disadvantage of such high levels of lighting – accentuated by the reflection of the river and the ceiling lights – was a rather cold,

blue-grey atmosphere. Warm cherry-wood finishes were used for work surfaces and partitions to combat the clinical ambience.

In making the move, certain difficulties inevitably arose, including the establishment of good relations between newly juxtaposed departments and the need for changes in internal organisation. Some staff had problems adapting to the open layout, while subsequent operational changes meant part of the office did, as predicted, have to be rearranged. Nevertheless, the installation proved a success in many ways – its flexibility, storage facilities, and efficient cable management gave the bank excellent room for manoeuvre. In addition, the whole office was installed in just four weekends, and the functional, pleasant surroundings were much appreciated by staff who had previously been working in conditions that were far from satisfactory.

4   XENOTRON

Hemel Hempstead, England
Business: providing computer-aided
photocomposition
Objective of the installation: to provide
flexbility for future evolution
One hundred workstations were instal-
led in an office space of 1,750sq m
(18,840sq ft), each featuring a compu-
ter terminal. A combination of top and
task lighting was used in the installa-
tion, which was completed in January
1988.
Layout: 85 per cent open plan, 15 per
cent closed.

The Xenotron company was
founded at the beginning of the
1980s, and had grown to employ
120 staff. Its business, computer-
based photosetting, was undertaken mainly for the publishing
industry. Rapid expansion had
led to the doubling of business
over the previous two years.

CHALLENGES OF THE INSTALLATION

Based in eastern England, the company decided that a move nearer London would be vital to its future success; the market was becoming more competitive, and most of Xenotron's customers were in the south-east. Relocation would create a number of problems, not least convincing a highly qualified workforce – who were not afraid of finding another employer – to leave homes, relatives and friends. Staff were also concerned that living costs would be significantly higher in the new location.

To counter such problems, Xenotron needed to be able to offer very attractive work conditions, and this became the number one objective. A Hemel Hempstead business park was chosen as the new site. Northeast of London and with good transport links, the area also offered the important advantage of a lower cost of living than most other London suburbs. The building itself, provided fully finished, had a U-shaped plan wrapped around a central atrium.

Office layout was entrusted to a professional, who started with a blank sheet of paper, the only constraints being the budget and a tight timescale. Four requirements guided the installation. First, the company expected to grow, so the scheme had to be flexible enough to allow subsequent reorganisation. Secondly, a large amount of computer hardware had to be accommodated. The plan had to make the most of the light entering offices from the atrium, and finally, a use had to be defined for the atrium.

SOLUTION

Departments most likely to require electronic equipment were arranged at ground level, where a raised floor was installed to facilitate easy wiring. To maintain good lighting, spaces were semi-partitioned, although a few cellular offices were provided on the first floor for some executives, after consultation. The atrium was considered unsuitable for office use as people in it would be 'on show' and could be looked down on by others. The idea of covering it over at first-floor level was also dismissed as it would cut light entering surrounding areas. In-

stead, it was turned into a reception area at one end, and the remainder was furnished in a relaxed, exotic manner to provide a space for parties and informal get-togethers.

Xenotron's objectives were largely met and staff were positive from the start. Before moving in, they were given a detailed briefing and invited to visit their new premises – an invitation accepted by all but one of the staff. Some reservations were expressed about the semi-open offices, as people feared a loss of privacy. But, once workstations were personalised, most staff said they were happy with the installation. Customers, too, found much to praise in the new offices and their comments were greeted with pride and satisfaction by personnel.

5   MERCEDES–BENZ

142

Bremen-Sebaldsbruck, *West Germany*
Business: motor industry
Objective of installation: to centralise administrative functions, optimising floorspace and improving lighting and cable management
Two phases of installation – the first in late 1987 involving 480 staff in 6,800sq m (73,200sq ft) of offices, and the second in September 1989, installing 715 staff in 11,000sq m (118,400sq ft) of additional space. Ambient and localised lighting, with a visual display unit at each workstation.
Layout: 85 per cent open, 15 per cent closed.

The Bremen plant is one of 11 locations occupied by Mercedes in West Germany. About 16,000 workers are based at the site, which produces three different sorts of cars: the 190 series, the station wagon (200TD–300TE) and the new Roadster (300SL–500SL). Acquired by the company in 1978, the plant did not come with an administrative block, but contained only isolated offices dotted about the plant. Temporary office buildings were built during the 1980s, where the site permitted, to meet the need for space.

This organisation of the plant generated heavy costs, with real communication problems between departments, despite the use of additional messengers. Ultimately, the need for a new administrative centre was accepted, especially as it was clear that production activities needed more space on the existing site.

The original offices were not difficult to improve on. Although some workstations were equipped with terminals, lighting and acoustic inadequacies aggravated staff. The legibility of the screen was also reduced by the reflected daylight and ceiling lighting, while noise from adjacent production shops distracted concentration. The company also accepted that the ageing infrastructure would make installation of a new communication network a major problem.

Mercedes therefore considered the possibility of erecting a new building. Specifications were drawn up by a specially created work team assisted by a consulting group of the Quickborner team: they took account of provisional data, functional relations, likely changes in the medium term, and the standards of working environment required for different types of work. A full economic study was also completed.

SOLUTION

The new building was designed to meet future needs from the outset. All staff were ultimately to have a computer terminal, with two-thirds acquiring them when they moved in. So raised floors were installed throughout, providing the flexibility for additional wiring.

The general plans, management of volumes and furniture were determined according to existing work patterns. Work groups consisted of between 5 and 12 people who needed to be placed together; this, and acoustic, lighting and furnishing requirements, resulted in the use of cellular offices for only 15 per cent of the space, with the remainder organised in a semi-open layout. The combination also provided maximum flexibility, should future alterations be necessary.

A dual lighting system, featuring ambient and task fittings, was

chosen and adapted to the needs of individual workstations. The specification called for ambient lighting and wiring to be integrated into the furniture, both for aesthetic and functional

144

reasons. Computer, electrical and telephone wires were carried to workstations beneath the raised floor. A central heating system and forced ventilation were deemed sufficient to pro-vide thermal comfort; full air-conditioning was not consi-dered desirable by staff, who were given windows close to workstations that they could open if necessary.

The installation clearly solved the company's problems. Grouping the various depart-ments together increased their efficiency considerably and brought tangible improvements

146

in individuals' working environments. The installation met current requirements, as well as providing ample flexibility for future changes. The ingenious combination of collective offices and small conference rooms also brought about improved communications.

One short-term problem, however, was the lack of enthusiasm shown by some staff for the semi-open space, with which they were not familiar. Nevertheless, they soon began to appreciate the advantages of this system, particularly the way in which it provided intimacy and allowed for better working concentration.

6 RHONE–POULENC

Antony, France
Business: human and animal health
Objective of installation: to integrate new technology and improve working conditions
A total of 900 workstations installed, with a visual display unit at each, in three phases: 4,000sq m (43,000sq ft) in March 1987, 7,000sq m (75,350sq ft) in April 1988, and 10,000sq m (107,640sq ft) in September 1989.
Layout: half open, half closed.

The introduction of a decentralised organisation meant that Rhone-Poulenc needed to set up a new head office for each of its four principal activities. For the health division, this created a need for new offices to bring together research and development staff, located at Antony, and administrative staff based in Paris. A new building was constructed on the Antony site to provide the required office space.

CHALLENGES OF THE INSTALLATION

Management were aware that the move and change of environment could prove disruptive, so their first concern was to offer as compensation a working environment that was not only functional and in line with the company's dynamic requirements, but also met with staff approval.

Staff had made it clear that their previous offices in Paris were far from ideal. The building was dark – people had nicknamed it 'the submarine' – with long corridors deprived of natural light, security partitioning, cellular offices and 10-year-old furniture which was ill-suited to the demands of office automation. The cellular structure, with automatic door closers provided for security reasons, had posed serious communication problems, although it was acceptable acoustically.

Major objectives of the installation therefore included adapting to new technology and meeting communication needs, both in terms of overall space management, and at individual workstations. More than half of the 900 employees were, from the outset, called upon to work at screens. Workstations had to be flexible enough to meet the needs of different departments and the various types of equipment used.

'The first requirement was that it should provide each workstation with a pleasant and dynamic environment, and facilitate communication between people,' according to the general manager at Antony. 'This was achieved through different harmonies of bright and young colours specific to each floor, and by glass panels which let natural light into the building, as well as allowing many visual contacts. In conjunction with the architect of the building, it had been agreed to combine collective semi-open spaces with individual cellular offices.'

150

SOLUTION

Preliminary studies suggested the use of modular furniture, and 10 manufacturers were asked to tender for the project. Three were shortlisted, and submitted a typical secretarial workstation, which was scrutinised by personnel during a site visit. A survey among future users was also undertaken, after which the company selected the preferred equipment.

Rhone-Poulenc then asked the manufacturer, Steelcase Strafor, to act as installation adviser. A list of workstation types was assembled, and discussion with staff ensured that future users understood the options, and made their requirements known. In less than five months, the study was completed, and 200 workstations were installed. Success with this phase led to the same approach being adopted for two further stages.

A mixed concept was adopted throughout: cellular offices were chosen for those whose functions demanded isolation and

confidentiality, while semi-open spaces were given to those requiring easy communication. Throughout, the building's luminosity was preserved by using part-glass panels, rather than full-height partitions, which also allowed corridors to be lit indirectly. A range of worktops was used, with panel-mounted filing space throughout. The use of modular elements showed its worth later, when other departments were moved to the site, or partial reorganisations carried out.

152

A satisfactory result was achieved through consideration of the users' opinion, and the efficient use of the installation. Staff appreciated that they had been given well-conceived offices that improved their comfort, facilitated the carrying out of their work and helped internal communication, as well as being light, functional and attractive.

7 STEELCASE

Michigan, United States
Business: the office environment
company
Objective of installation: to bring together branches of the business in a location that would enhance research and development of new products
A 57,000 sq m (614,000 sq ft) building houses 33,000 sq m (355,000 sq ft) of office space, with the remainder devoted to support services and laboratories. The building accommodates 809 staff, who were moved into the building in early 1989.
Layout: predominantly open plan.

CHALLENGES OF THE INSTALLATION

Steelcase decided that it needed to enhance its market position. The key to this would be reducing the time taken to develop new products, something only possible if staff were more creative and innovative. The catalyst in achieving this would be bringing together those involved in the development process to work more closely together, creating new teams, in a new Corporate Development Center.

The disparate departments, such as marketing, research and development, engineering, industrial design and manufacturing, needed to be able to communicate effectively, and share a great deal of information to make anything of their juxtaposi-

tion. Theories suggested that an improvement in creativity was linked to the frequency of human contact with people outside an individual's working group – so an office layout had to create opportunities for accidental contact, by the use of 'functional inconvenience' in planning. This approach contrasted with the simplistic method of laying out an office, which would place those with frequent working contact close together, for the sake of efficiency.

The company also recognised that putting groups of people with such different ideologies together in a uniform layout of offices would make them all uncomfortable. With creativity featuring highly in the work of the staff, the new offices had to be appropriate for informality, relaxation and reflection, in recognition that all these activities could enhance the enigmatic creative process.

SOLUTION

With such a large number of people requiring to be close together, the form of the new building was of vital importance. Initially, an L-shaped building was envisaged, but research into communication between staff suggested that people placed too far apart, even in the same building, would not communicate with one another either on a face-to-face basis or by the use of telephones or computers. So a pyramidal form was chosen instead – ensuring that everyone was within a critical proximity to other parts of the building. The allocation of space was achieved so that departments requiring large areas in which to work together, for instance, in the design laboratories, were located near the base of the pyramid, with smaller teams of people occupying the more confined upper storeys.

The form of the Corporate Development Center building introduced elements to support the aims of the project; escalators were used, for example, instead of stairs or lifts, to increase the individual's awareness of others, and improve communication. While an atrium was used to house an informal meeting area, this was deliberately separated from the view of visitors, to prevent any feeling of being on show.

The office space provided a variety of areas for individuals.

Workstations were grouped together, with a variety of other shared facilities including project and conference rooms, coffee break areas, etc. These shared rooms were placed throughout the building, requiring travel from the workstation to get to a meeting, establishing functional inconvenience. In addition to such spaces, common room-style areas were also provided. The furniture in these spaces was easy to rearrange to encourage individuals and groups to use them for anything from informal gatherings to presentation and display areas.

An information library was set up separately and provided with work cubicles, should individuals need periods of quiet for

intense concentration. And management staff from the different disciplines were grouped together in the centre of the building, encouraging them to communicate with one another, and improving their accessibility to staff.

Throughout the installation process, staff were involved in the design and layout of floors and their working areas, and were involved with briefings, information sheets and discussions both before and after the move. In addition, a 'tenants' council' was set up to ensure that any problems in the running of the building were ironed out as soon as they became apparent.

157

158

INDEX